6.95

FIFTY
COMMON
BIRDS OF
OKLAHOMA
AND THE
SOUTHERN GREAT PLAINS

D0907474

The University of Oklahoma Press : Norman

FIFTY
COMMON
BIRDS OF
OKLAHOMA
AND THE
SOUTHERN GREAT PLAINS

GEORGE MIKSCH
SUTTON

BY GEORGE MIKSCH SUTTON

Portraits of Mexican Birds: Fifty Selected Paintings (Norman, 1975)
At a Bend in a Mexican River (New York, 1972)
High Arctic (New York, 1971)
Oklahoma Birds: Their Ecology and Distribution, with Comments on the Avifauna of the Southern Great Plains (Norman, 1967)
Iceland Summer: Adventures of a Bird Painter (Norman, 1961, 1974)
Mexican Birds: First Impressions (Norman, 1951)
Birds in the Wilderness (New York, 1936)
Eskimo Year (New York, 1934)
The Exploration of Southampton Island, Hudson Bay (Pittsburgh, 1932)
An Introduction to the Birds of Pennsylvania (Harrisburg, 1928)

ILLUSTRATED BY GEORGE MIKSCH SUTTON

A Guide to the Birds of South America (in part) (by R. Meyer de Schauensee) (Wynnewood, 1970)
The Birds of Colombia (in part) (by R. Meyer de Schauensee) (Narbeth, 1964)
The Birds of Arizona (by Allan Phillips, Joe Marshall, and Gale Monson) (Tucson, 1964)
Fundamentals of Ornithology (by Josselyn Van Tyne and Andrew J. Berger) (New York, 1959)
Georgia Birds (Norman, 1958)
A Guide to Bird Finding West of the Mississippi (by Olin Sewall Pettingill Jr.) (New York, 1953)
A Guide to Bird Finding East of the Mississippi (by Olin Sewall Pettingill Jr.) (New York, 1951)
World Book Encyclopedia (section on birds) (Chicago, 1941)
Birds of Western Pennsylvania (by W. E. C. Todd) (Pittsburgh, 1940)
The Golden Plover and Other Birds (by A. A. Allen) (Ithaca, 1939)
Wings, Fur and Shot (by Robert B. Vale) (Harrisburg, 1936)
American Bird Biographies (by A. A. Allen) (Ithaca, 1934)
The Birds of Minnesota (in part) (by T. S. Roberts) (Minneapolis, 1932)
The Burgess Seashore Book (in part) (by Thornton Burgess) (Boston, 1929)
The Birds of Florida (by H. H. Bailey) (Baltimore, 1925)
Our Bird Friends and Foes (by William Atherton Dupuy) (Philadelphia, 1925)

Library of Congress Cataloging in Publication Data

Sutton, George Miksch, 1898–
    Fifty common birds of Oklahoma and the southern Great Plains.

    1. Birds—Oklahoma. 2. Birds—Great Plains. 3. Birds—Pictorial works. I. Title.
QL684.05S79   598.2'9766   77–24336

Copyright © 1977 by the University of Oklahoma Press, Norman, Publishing Division of the University of Oklahoma. Manufactured in the U.S.A. First edition, 1977; second printing, 1978; third printing, 1981.

FOREWORD

When it became clear to me that a book of this sort would help to acquaint Oklahomans with the wealth of their state's birdlife, I was faced immediately with the problem of deciding which fifty birds to include. People living in heavily forested parts of southeastern Oklahoma may so frequently see or hear that glorious crow-sized red, black, and white woodpecker known in scientific circles as the Pileated Woodpecker *(Dryocopus pileatus)*—and among "crackers" of Georgia and Florida as the "Lord God" or even the "Lord God Almighty"—that they think of it as common; yet in central Oklahoma the species is decidedly uncommon, and west of Alfalfa, Major, and Comanche counties it has never even been seen. By the same token, residents of Boise City, at the west end of the Panhandle, have but to drive to the Cimarron River 13 miles north of town to see the Black-billed Magpie *(Pica pica)*, a species that has been reported only a few times from anywhere east of the Panhandle. The Pileated Woodpecker and Black-billed Magpie are both well worth knowing, the more so since they are truly Oklahoma birds rather than casual wanderers from afar; but in this book the accent must, in my opinion, be on birds that may be seen in any part of the state.

So which of Oklahoma's some four hundred kinds of birds (see list, page 103) are to be the "elect" fifty? Which are truly the commonest? And which have a right to be widely known even though restricted to a certain sort of habitat or findable only at certain seasons?

After discussing the matter with certain members of the Oklahoma Ornithological Society, I decided that the Common Crow *(Corvus brachyrhynchos)* should not be one of the fifty. The decision was not easy, partly because the crow has long been one of my favorite birds, and partly because good coverage of the Common Crow might well include comment about the White-necked Raven *(C. cryptoleucus)*, a well known corvid of western Oklahoma; the Fish Crow *(C. ossifragus)*, a small, very glossy crow that has made its way up the Arkansas and Red rivers to heronries in eastern Oklahoma; and the big Common Raven *(C. corax)*, which nests in considerable numbers in the Black Mesa country at the northwestern corner of the Panhandle. All three of these congeners of the Common Crow deserve to be better known than they are.

Too, what about those three Old World species that have made themselves so conspicuously at home in America—the domestic pigeon or Rock Dove *(Columba livia)*, which nests not only in cities and about ranch buildings but also on cliffs and about bridges and caves well away from towns, though I know of no "wild" Oklahoma population whose every bird has the fine coloration of the ancestral stock; the Starling *(Sturnus vulgaris)*, a tough, aggressive bird, whose stealing of nest-holes is eliminating certain woodpeckers from the scene; and the

House (or English) Sparrow *(Passer domesticus)*, a remarkably intelligent little creature whose adaptability deserves careful study. Should any of these be among the chosen fifty?

Surely everyone everywhere must know the barnyard pigeon. So my vote on the Rock Dove is an unequivocal *no*. As for the Starling, that slightly-smaller-than-a-robin species is common statewide, especially in towns, but many people who see it, even those who see it many times each day, have only a vague idea as to what it is. "What are those chunky looking birds that we see on our lawn? They waddle when they walk. Their bills look yellow and their tail is short." Answering, I explain that the Starling's bill is yellow when the annual reproductive cycle starts, but dark from the end of the nesting season until the following spring. "The Starling is actually rather pretty," I continue. "Its head and body feathers are highly iridescent except for the white at the tip, so the bird has a fine green and purple shine when the sun strikes it. The white tips wear off as the season advances, so by midsummer, about the time the molt starts, Starlings may be quite black. They are less glossy, too, than they were in spring." This time the vote again is *no*, but the *no* is less positive. I content myself with the decision, realizing that what is said above describes the bird a bit.

The House Sparrow should, perhaps, be among the "select fifty." Assuredly it is among the most abundant of Oklahoma's birds and it has become pretty thoroughly Americanized. It is commoner by far in towns and about farm buildings than in the woods; but I have seen it in flocks along highways far from towns in treeless parts of the Panhandle, where it was finding shelter in the shaggy masses of tumbleweed that had accumulated along the fences. When I first observed these flocks I was sincerely puzzled. Could *House* Sparrows possibly be so numerous miles away from the nearest houses? House Sparrows indeed they were, and I was impressed with the way in which they were finding shelter in and under the masses of tumbleweed and feeding in the wide fields of stubble. In that part of Oklahoma the House Sparrow often builds its bulky, domed-over nest in a tree close to the highway.

Another fact about the House Sparrow must be mentioned. In the many "specimen quizzes" that I have given while teaching ornithology during the past fifty years, the bird most often missed has been the female House Sparrow. This was, I suppose, because the students assumed that I would not quiz them on anything so "dirt common" as the House Sparrow; but it might also have been because they had never paid close attention to the drab little thing that the female House Sparrow admittedly is. People seem to remember what the black-throated, rather handsome adult male *Passer domesticus* looks like; but his mate is utterly nondescript and therefore not quite deserving of close attention. So the vote on the House Sparrow is *no*; but reaching that decision was not easy.

It will surprise some readers to learn how many of Oklahoma's commonest birds are virtually unknown in this part of the world. A good example is the Nashville Warbler *(Vermivora ruficapilla)*, a species that comparatively few persons have ever heard of, that fewer still can identify with assurance, but one that migrates through Oklahoma by the thousand every spring and every fall. Held in the hand, it is attractive, but it moves through the leafage so rapidly that no one gets a very good look at it. Its song in spring is not at all noticeable; and most people who see it dismiss it as "one of those little wild canaries," making no effort to find what its name is. On one fall morning in 1974, near the town of Coweta, in northeastern Oklahoma, James L. Norman picked up the bodies of sixty-four Nashville Warblers that had killed themselves by flying into a TV tower at night. The Nashville Warbler has been seen in more than half of the seventy-seven counties of the state—from Adair and LeFlore in the east to Cimarron in the west. It does not nest here, nor does it winter, but it is one of our commonest birds—hence its inclusion in this book.

Two other species that migrate through Oklahoma in great numbers, though they do not nest here, are the Swainson's Thrush *(Catharus ustulatus)* and Lincoln's Sparrow *(Melospiza lincolnii)*. Another species, the Harris's Sparrow *(Zonotrichia querula)*, is in a slightly different category: it is common as a transient and also as a winter resident, though its breeding grounds are a thousand miles or so north of Oklahoma.

Our official state bird, the Scissor-tailed Flycatcher *(Muscivora forficata)*, is far from equally common in all parts of Oklahoma. It is uncommon to rare throughout most of the Panhandle. Yet east of the Panhandle it is so common in certain areas of open pastureland and it is everywhere so much admired and talked about, that leaving it out of a work of this sort would be unforgivable. The Roadrunner *(Geococcyx californianus)*, though nowhere really plentiful in Oklahoma, is found widely in small numbers even in rather heavily wooded areas and along railroad right-of-ways in towns. Leaving the Roadrunner out would be another mistake.

Several species are surely among Oklahoma's most often observed birds, but their abundance varies seasonally and from place to place. Great numbers of Swainson's Hawks *(Buteo swainsoni)* and Franklin's Gulls *(Larus pipixcan)* pass through the state on their way southward to far-removed wintering grounds and northward to their summer home. Some of the Swainson's Hawks nest here, but most of them do not. Great flocks of Ring-billed Gulls *(Larus delawarensis)* gather at certain impoundments in winter when cold weather kills thousands of fish. Hordes of shorebirds, especially the small species known as "peeps," stop to feed on mud flats, giving bird students a chance to test their knowledge. One "peep," the Least Sandpiper *(Calidris minutilla)*, is in a very special category: though never extremely abundant, it is among the very few birds that do not nest anywhere in Oklahoma but may be seen during virtually every week of the year. Such continuing occurrence of a species that is not truly "resident" is a bit difficult to explain. Least Sandpipers seen in Oklahoma in June probably have not migrated to their breeding grounds—but what has kept them from doing so? Finding the answers to questions of this sort is part of what keeps bird students busy and happy.

Among birds that might well have been discussed in this book, but that rather arbitrarily had to be excluded, are the Great Blue Heron *(Ardea herodias)*, Green Heron *(Butorides striatus)*, Canada Goose *(Branta canadensis)*, Turkey Vulture *(Cathartes aura)*, Bobwhite *(Colinus virginianus)*, Screech Owl *(Otus asio)*, Belted Kingfisher *(Megaceryle alcyon)*, Red-headed Woodpecker *(Melanerpes erythrocephalus)*, Horned Lark *(Eremophila alpestris)*, Mockingbird *(Mimus polyglottos)*, Brown Thrasher *(Toxostoma rufum)*, Blue Grosbeak *(Guiraca caerulea)*, and Lark Sparrow *(Chondestes grammacus)*. A bird of prey that is found statewide in winter and that nests in scattered low-lying areas is the Marsh Hawk *(Circus cyaneus)*. The best known of Oklahoma's wild ducks probably is the Mallard *(Anas platyrhynchos)*, a species that breeds widely in the state, though in small numbers. An equally common, but less well known, duck is the Blue-winged Teal *(A. discors)*. The Wild Turkey *(Meleagris gallopavo)*, as a result of successful restocking and good management, has become remarkably common in many areas. Should another book of this sort be brought out, the above-mentioned birds would surely be among those discussed and portrayed.

In the interest of helping the novice to locate Oklahoma birds in their natural habitat, I cannot close this foreword without discussing "the squeak," a sound produced by kissing the back of the hand, or the palm, in imitation of the cry of a terrified or injured nestling. To "squeak" effectively requires practice. Hide yourself well in a thicket or under vines before starting. Take a position and remain motionless. Then put yourself into the performance, making it sound genuine. *Feel* a bit terrified yourself. And don't give up too quickly. Birds have good ears. They may hear you though they're a hundred yards away. Little birds that usually respond quickly and come close are the Blue-gray Gnatcatcher *(Polioptila caerulea)*, Ruby-crowned Kinglet *(Regulus calendula)*, and Field Sparrow *(Spizella pusilla)*; but a hawk, owl, fox, or bobcat may be impelled to investigate, so be ready for anything.

What you pull in will depend largely on where you are. If you're in a park or wooded part of town, you may call a Northern Oriole *(Icterus galbula)* down from the treetops. This time, if your "victim" happens to be a fully adult male, you'll have a brief look at one of our handsomest birds.

Finally, a word of thanks. Several of the drawings reproduced here were made for the late W. E. Clyde Todd's scholarly *Birds of Western Pennsylvania*, published in 1940 by the University of Pittsburgh Press. These drawings, now owned by the Carnegie Museum of Natural History in Pittsburgh, were lent through the kind offices of M. Graham Netting, formerly the Director of that institution, and of Kenneth C. Parkes, the Curator of Birds there. Several other drawings, first reproduced in an early edition of *The World Book Encyclopedia* and now the property of the Field Enterprises Educational Corporation of Chicago, were lent through the courtesy of William J. Dobias, Vice-president and Executive Art Director of that corporation. I am deeply grateful to the three named gentlemen for their help.

GEORGE MIKSCH SUTTON

CONTENTS

FIFTY
COMMON
BIRDS OF
OKLAHOMA
AND THE
SOUTHERN GREAT PLAINS

MISSISSIPPI KITE *(Ictinia mississippiensis)*

The Mississippi Kite is downright common in parts of western Oklahoma today. The eastern limits of its breeding are in Kay, Payne, Oklahoma, and Comanche counties chiefly, but it has reared young in Tulsa County recently and sightings in Osage, Pawnee, Creek, Washington, Muskogee, Cleveland, Pottawatomie, and Murray counties suggest that it may be moving back into those areas. In the shinnery oak country of Ellis and Roger Mills counties it is a familiar summer bird.

The kite likes warm weather: return from the south as early as April 9 is exceptional; by mid-September most of the kites have gone. When breeding pairs settle down for the season, they circle peaceably over the tree-dotted cattle range, perching now and then not far apart on high dead stubs, occasionally catching a large insect and eating it while on the wing. They are a pale shade of gray on the head, a bit darker on the back and underparts, darker still on the wings and tail. The white tips of the inner wing feathers form a bar on the following edge that is a good field mark. As they circle, the fanned tail tilts now this way, now that, without seeming to affect the direction of flight. In each spread wing of the male a chestnut patch shows more or less clearly.

Nests are in cottonwood, hackberry, elm, or locust trees from 15 to 30 feet up, as a rule. One that I found in the summer of 1936 was in a shinnery oak only about 6 feet from the ground. It was so low that I could look down into it from horseback, and so confiding was the incubating bird that I could almost touch her *if I stayed on the horse.* If I dismounted, she and her mate dived at me fiercely, crying *phee-phew* in a shrill voice.

The eggs, usually two, are pale bluish white. They are incubated for about a month. The newly-hatched downy chick is white, with a tinge of buff on the upperparts and a light gray mask between the bill and eye. The chicks remain in the nest a long while. The food brought to them is cicadas, grasshoppers, and camel crickets chiefly.

When the young are ready to fledge, they are not much like the old birds in color. Their underparts are white, boldly streaked with brown; their upperparts dark brown streaked with rufous, buff, and white; their tail blackish brown boldly barred with white.

In the summer of 1936 I made a close study of the kites with my headquarters at the old Scott Hotel in Arnett. A game ranger there told me of shooting twenty-two of the lovely birds, one after the other, as they alighted on the very same stub. He argued that shooting them was a good thing, for they were known to destroy "a lot of baby quail and prairie chickens." The stomachs of specimens that I collected contained insects almost exclusively, though one held the remains of a lizard. Mark Ports, who studied the kites in Oklahoma City during the summer of 1976, found evidence that Chimney Swifts were occasionally fed to the young kites.

3

RED-TAILED HAWK *(Buteo jamaicensis)*

The Red-tailed Hawk of Oklahoma is difficult to describe, for one race or geographical subspecies with comparatively unmarked underparts when fully adult breeds here and often winters; a black or almost black race regularly winters; and two or three additional races show up irregularly during the season of migration or in winter. Adult individuals of the race that breeds here are really red-tailed, the red being of a rich, orange-brick shade that shows clearly when the flying bird circles in such a way as to reveal its top-side now and then. In young birds the tail is *gray*, crossed by several dark bands. Young birds differ markedly from their parents, too, in that their underparts may be heavily marked with black. In the all-black race that winters here, a form long considered a separate species, and known as the Harlan's Hawk, the feathers of the chin, throat, and chest are white basally and the tail is gray, not red. The tail's markings in adults are dark marblings that run the long way of the feathers, in young birds, many dark bars with herring-bone effect.

Red-tail nests that I have found in eastern and central Oklahoma have all been well up in large trees; but in the rough Black Mesa country at the west end of the Panhandle, nests are usually on cliffs. When pairs are forming in early spring, the two birds circle majestically, sometimes so high as to be almost out of sight. Their thin, shrill screams drift down without seeming to come from anything but sky. The hawks build their own nest, a huge mass of sticks set in a sustantial fork. A nest may be used several times, not necessarily in successive years. The two or three eggs are white or very pale bluish green, either immaculate or speckled lightly with brown. Only the female incubates, but her mate brings food to her while she is on the eggs. The incubation period lasts twenty-eight to thirty days.

Red-tails live largely on rodents from cottontail-size down. In the Black Mesa country, on October 1, 1932, I saw an adult Red-tail catch a young prairie dog. I was close to the Cimarron River at the time, hidden from the hawk by a high bank. The hawk set its wing and glided swiftly downward directly over me. At first I had no idea that it was after anything; then I saw that it was headed for a mound at the edge of a dog-town a hundred yards away. When it struck, a cloud of dust rose. I could not tell what was happening, though the great bird appeared to tumble over. Presently the dust settled and off the hawk flew, carrying its kicking prey.

AMERICAN KESTREL *(Falco sparverius)*

This handsome little New World falcon has been widely known as the Sparrow Hawk, an unacceptable name, since an Old World hawk of a very different sort has for centuries been called that. The American Kestrel resembles the Eurasian Kestrel *(F. tinnunculus)* in several ways. Both species are given to hanging in one spot in the air with wings rapidly beating while they scan the ground for prey, a habit that has won for the Old World bird the pretty name Windhover.

Our kestrel eats grasshoppers chiefly; but it also catches field mice, lizards, small snakes, and now and then a bird. A pet kestrel that I had as a teen-ager captured sparrows that fed near a certain barn. My pet would approach along one side of the building, turn the corner sharply, and snatch the fleeing sparrow from the air.

Falco sparverius breeds widely in North and South America and the West Indies. In the fall it moves southward from Canada and the northern United States into the southern states and Mexico. Birds that breed in Oklahoma may be replaced by birds from the north in winter, but I suspect that they are not. Indeed, with the coming of cool weather kestrels become so common on wires and poles along our highways that I cannot help feeling that what we are seeing is birds that have bred here and their progeny *plus* birds from the north.

American Kestrels can be remarkably secretive during the nesting season. At least one pair has bred in or close to Norman every year since my moving here in the fall of 1952, yet I have failed to find their nest. I might have felt that the birds were merely "hanging around" had someone not brought me a stub-tailed nestling, far too young to fly, that had fallen from a building on the university campus.

Throughout most of Oklahoma the kestrel nests in cavities in trees, but in the Black Mesa country it often nests in crevices in cliffs. One nest that I found in that part of the state was in an old iron bridge. When I climbed for a look at the eggs, I was surprised that no bird dived at me. Had I not seen the bird fly from that one particular place, I'd never have climbed to it.

The characteristic cry of our kestrel, a spirited *killy* or *killee* repeated rapidly, is responsible for the colloquial name Killy Hawk. At Cornell University some years ago, someone brought a brood of baby Killy Hawks to my office. They were sorry looking little things when I took them from the gunny sack, but they perked up when given some water and, to my surprise, took bits of meat from my fingers as if quite used to such an oversized provider as I. While being fed they let out a volley of *killees* that made the halls ring. Their nest-tree had blown over during a storm.

Courtesy Field Enterprises Educational Corporation.

7

KILLDEER *(Charadrius vociferus)*

This New World plover is among the most easily recognized of Oklahoma's birds. Its white underparts are crossed by two black chestbands; the orange-brown of its rump is a good field mark; and its call is a clearly enunciated *kill-dee*. Bird students intent on studying other shorebirds that are feeding on a big mud flat can be annoyed by the Killdeer's shrill cries, for these warn one and all that danger is at hand.

Killdeers nest on flat ground in the open, often well away from water and often without a blade of grass to shelter the eggs from rain, sun, and wind. I have seen nests in the middle of a dirt road, on a highway shoulder within inches of the pavement, and in a bare spot not far from third base of a baseball diamond. A Killdeer incubating its eggs is obliged to leave them when almost stepped on, so off it runs with tail spread wide and bright rump-patch gleaming. Now, crying pitifully, it drags itself along as if badly crippled, or falls to one side with the other wing feebly flapping. The ruse often succeeds, for persons not "in the know" chase the bird, feeling sure that they can catch it. The bird student, however, soon finds the nest with its four speckled eggs. They are hard to see, for they look like gravel. Each has its small end pointed inward and down. Packed in as they are, they can all be covered by the incubating bird. They are very large. The newly hatched chicks are so well developed that they leave the nest soon after their downy plumage has dried.

Without the eggs the nest appears to be a shallow cup that just happens to be there; but I have watched Killdeers gathering little pebbles and lining the "scrape" with considerable care. A nest that I found long ago in Pennsylvania was surrounded with black bits of charred wood. The area thereabouts had been burned-over the preceding winter, so plenty of charred bits were available, but the mosaic around the nest was no accident.

Several Oklahoma nests that I have known about were on the flat gravelled tops of low buildings. At nests of this sort, I suspect that the female lays the eggs without any attempt to make a nest. How the chicks get to the ground remains to be ascertained. I suspect that they fall off rather than being carried down. If the roof is enclosed by a wall, I have no idea how the chicks get over it. Some patient photographer may find out some day.

Both male and female Killdeer incubate the eggs. The incubation period is from twenty-five to twenty-eight days. The downy young are so protectively colored that if they crouch and remain motionless they are very hard to see. The down at their tail end is black and exceedingly long. This often adheres for weeks to the tips of the incoming feathers of the first winter plumage.

MOURNING DOVE *(Zenaida macroura)*

Many a bird student has wondered how the Mourning Dove, which is extremely popular as game in Oklahoma, can continue to be among our commonest birds. Its flocks are never as large as the blackbird flocks that roost near Oklahoma City, nor does it foregather in hordes in one area winter after winter as do the crows at Fort Cobb Reservoir. But the sum total of all the flocks of doves that feed and roost together in fall and winter, especially in southwestern Oklahoma, must be immense—to say nothing of the thousands of pairs that breed throughout the state.

No one knows how many of the doves that are shot each fall in Oklahoma have actually bred or been reared here. Many are surely from north of Oklahoma, for the species is strongly migratory. The extent to which our doves may move about is clearly indicated by the fact that one dove banded as a nestling in northwestern Oklahoma was recovered as far away as Jalisco, in southwestern Mexico.

In its breeding the Mourning Dove is exceedingly adaptable. It nests not only in heavily forested areas but in areas that have no trees at all. Studies have shown that even where nest sites in trees are available, almost half of the doves nest on the ground. I have observed such a population in open woods along the Beaver River 5 miles northeast of Guymon, in the Panhandle. There, to my surprise, I found that nests on the ground were producing as many young as nests above ground—a circumstance hard to explain. Many doves nest in towns. Here broods may have a greater chance to survive than those in the wild, since such predators as snakes are missing from the towns, and since the force of the wind is cut down by houses and other buildings. Dove nests are notoriously flimsy; many of them are destroyed during storms.

The dove's urge to reproduce is amazing. Only two young are reared at a nesting, but in this comparatively southern part of the breeding range, three, four, even five broods may be reared in a summer. Pairs form early, egg-laying starts early, and the rearing of broods moves along at an astonishing pace. At a nest on the university campus here in Norman I saw a parent dove feed one of the two almost-fledged chicks, go to the ground for nest material, fly with this to a half-finished, much higher nest in a tree about 20 yards away, then return to brood the young. Eggs were in the new nest a week later.

The male and female work together building the nest, and both are faithful in tending the young, feeding them by regurgitation on a mixture of predigested food and a nutritious substance called "pigeon milk" that is secreted by the walls of the crop.

YELLOW-BILLED CUCKOO *(Coccyzus americanus)*

This bird is often called the Rain Crow—not a very good name, really, for cuckoos are not closely related to crows, nor does this species call only when it rains, has just rained, or is about to rain. I suspect that when a summer storm is gathering people become apprehensive, listen more carefully than usual, and hear more than they do most of the time. At any rate, off in the woods sounds the Rain Crow's slightly guttural *kuck-kuck-kuck-kuck, kelp, kelp, kelp, kelp*—a song I've always liked, for it brings to mind shady places that are pleasant no matter how hot the day.

Both the Yellow-billed Cuckoo and Black-billed Cuckoo *(C. erythropthalmus)* are Oklahoma birds. The Yellow-bill is far the commoner, however, and it nests statewide, whereas the Black-bill is known to have nested only in the northern half of the main body of the state. The Black-bill has no russet-brown on its wings and the white "thumb-marks" at the tips of its outer tail feathers are inconspicuous. In the Yellow-bill these "thumb-marks" are noticeable, especially when the bird flies.

Both the Yellow-bill and Black-bill are confirmed eaters of caterpillars. This does not mean that when webworms attack a tree in the yard some cuckoo will promptly come to the rescue. The fact is that Yellow-bills in town are exceptional, chiefly, I believe, because so many of them are hit by cars or killed by flying into windows. The Yellow-bill has never learned to fly high enough above highways to miss the stream of traffic. In the bird collection at the University of Oklahoma about half of the big trayful of Yellow-billed Cuckoo specimens were found dead under windows or on highways.

The eggs of the Yellow-bill are a fine pale blue. The nest is rather flat and flimsy, made of coarse twigs and lined with such soft materials as paper-thin leaf skeletons and dried catkins. The young at hatching are covered with light-gray hairlike feathers. These are pushed out promptly by the impatient blood quills, which remain fully sheathed for some time, giving the nestling the appearance of some kind of hedgehog. Comes the time when, simultaneously over the whole scrawny little body, the quills burst, and presto the young cuckoo "blooms," becoming quite presentable. The transformation can be truly spectacular, though only the dedicated bird student is ever patient enough to witness it.

In southwestern Georgia, in the early summer of 1952, I saw a Yellow-billed Cuckoo high in a tulip poplar tree catch a full grown lizard that was, tail and all, about as long as its captor. The cuckoo had quite a time killing and flying off with its prey. Its tactics called to mind those of its famous ground-inhabiting relative, the Roadrunner.

Courtesy the Carnegie Museum of Natural History.

ROADRUNNER *(Geococcyx californianus)*

The Roadrunner is far more widely distributed in Oklahoma than most people realize. It is slowly extending its range northward and eastward into Missouri and Arkansas. Known among cattlemen as the Chaparral, it is a creature about which many a tale has been told. One of these has the bird surrounding a rattler with prickly pear pads then so confusing it by darting at it that the snake is stabbed to death by the cactus spines.

I suspect that no rattler ever died from an overdose of cactus spines, but I know from repeated observation that Roadrunners are capable of capturing a wide variety of prey. Two birds that I reared as a kid in Texas combined forces in heading off and killing a cotton rat, flicked the legs from a tarantula until the huge spider could no longer jump, and killed snakes up to two feet long by whacking them against the ground. Arguments over the snakes tired the birds so badly that I was obliged to cut long snakes in two.

Most Roadrunners that we see in Oklahoma are hunting prey along a highway shoulder, and many that try crossing the stream of traffic are killed by cars. If an observer wants to see what Roadrunners really do, he should find a nest, ascertain what routes the parent birds follow while bringing in food, and watch from a hidden place. Presently he will see precisely how a Roadrunner eyes the return to the ground of a flying grasshopper, sneaks up slowly, then dashes forward with wings spread and snatches the fleeing insect from the air.

Roadrunner nests that I have found have been from 2 to about 18 feet from the ground. The highest was in an oak. A low one was in a very small juniper on a dry mesa-slope. The juniper was in such an exposed position that I could watch the comings and goings of the old birds. Some of the lizards that they brought in were surprisingly large, though none was a mountain boomer, and I never saw them bringing in a snake. A nestling Roadrunner that swallows a big lizard cannot possibly get it all down at one time, so the tail end sticks out while the front end is digested.

Among the creatures that "even scores up" with the Roadrunner is the coachwhip snake, full-grown individuals of which swallow whole broods of young Roadrunners despite the attacks of the parent birds— or perhaps while the old birds are away from the nest. I suspect that big hawks occasionally catch Roadrunners. My class and I once watched a Red-tail diving repeatedly at a Roadrunner in a plum thicket. The hawk made try after try, even lunging straight into the tangle, but the Roadrunner slipped through the brush far more swiftly than the hawk could, and finally it darted out and off to the safety of the woods while the hawk was extricating itself.

GREAT HORNED OWL *(Bubo virginianus)*

This powerful predator is fairly common throughout Oklahoma. Nowhere is it a familiar dooryard bird, but scattered pairs continue to inhabit woodland not far from ranch houses and busy highways, rearing their two or three young year after year despite the perils of the hunting season and the roar of traffic.

The big owl's ability to capture a variety of prey has much to do with its widespread distribution. Cottontail rabbits, squirrels, and smaller rodents are staple items in its diet, not to mention barnyard fowl, other birds, skunks, snakes, fish, frogs, and crayfish. Oklahoma landowners are rarely bothered by Great Horns, a reason for this being, I believe, that rabbits and cotton rats are so abundant that the owls have no need to go after poultry. But when I was State Ornithologist of Pennsylvania fifty years ago I received a steady stream of mail in defense of bounty payment for the big owls, and some of what I learned was interesting indeed. At one man's farm so many chickens were stolen that he set steel traps on several fenceposts. Next morning a trap was missing, chain and all, and so was another chicken. Then a morning or so later a trap on another post held an owl from whose "free" leg dangled the missing trap.

Great Horns usually lay their eggs in the old nest of a hawk or crow. Occasionally they nest in a hollow tree, on a cliff ledge, or on the ground in a cave. A nest that I found in Dewey County was about 15 feet from the ground almost directly under a Red-tailed Hawk's nest 70 feet up in the same tree. In situations of this sort, prey of various kinds is probably abundant, and some of the owl's hunting almost certainly is done at night while the Red-tails are asleep. Continuing availability of food may well determine how many birds of prey can occupy a given area side by side (whether amicably or not) year after year.

Great Horned Owls nest very early, sometimes laying their white, almost spherical eggs in February or late January. Only one brood is reared per year. When eggs are destroyed by crows, a second clutch, or even a third, may be laid. If reproduction is delayed in this way, the young fledge very late. Late young may be dependent on their parents for food at about the time the new breeding cycle gets under way. In early fall I once watched an old bird giving loud courtship hoots in answer to hoots from another patch of woods some distance away. The big owl's throat puffed up and its tail lifted each time it hooted. A young bird, able to fly but still dependent on its parents for food, flew to the old bird, begging peevishly. The parent, obviously annoyed, gave a sullen hoot and flew at the young bird swiftly, knocking it to the ground. There the young one remained, uninjured but bewildered, for several minutes. Finally the old bird flew off, and so did the young one, but in an opposite direction.

Courtesy Field Enterprises Educational Corporation.

COMMON NIGHTHAWK *(Chordeiles minor)*

Every fall, without fail, broken-winged nighthawks found in the streets are brought to me. Only one wing has been broken, but often it has been all but sheared from the body. The street-lights are to blame. The lights attract insects, and the nighthawks, feeding just below tree-top level, are in the very midst of the intricate web of utility wires. In and out of the glow they move, occasionally almost brushing the lights with their wings. The supply of insects is inexhaustible. The birds feed until their stomachs are packed. The more we see of their swift, head-long flight, the more we wonder why so few of them strike wires.

Companies of southward-migrating nighthawks that feed in this way do not hasten on. They find bare branches on which to rest during the day, sometimes lingering in town for a week or more. They are utterly silent. We wonder where they have come from. On fine evenings in late August we sometimes see great numbers of the birds circling southward high in air. A white spot shows on each wing. Their maneuvering is graceful—several slow wingbeats followed by a fluttering upward that may or may not accompany the capturing of prey. I have never seen comparably large numbers of nighthawks on their way northward. Spring arrival is of individuals or of small, loose-knit companies, and return is announced by the rasping *pee-yee* call from the sky. A bit later comes the power-dive with its roar of set wings, a spectacular courtship performance responsible for the common name *bull bat*. The displaying bird is usually above an open area in which it will nest.

A sizeable paved tract near the Norman airfield was a favored nesting spot for nighthawks a few years ago. The birds laid their two, heavily speckled eggs on the bare cement. Today that area is upgrown with salt cedar and other vegetation, so it no longer attracts the nighthawks. In the summer of 1961 we observed there a total of eighteen nestings between June 17 and the end of August. There were no nests, strictly speaking. The eggs were well away from the shelter of grass or weeds. Finding them was not difficult when several of us marched about abreast, covering the ground thoroughly. The incubating birds would fly up, someone would spot the eggs, and another symbol would be added to the map in the field notebook.

The high moments that summer came when we visited the half-grown chicks. The downy siblings would be side by side, with eyes almost closed. Undisturbed, they remained motionless; but touched even gently they would stand up on their short legs, spread their long, down-covered wings, open their mouths wide while emitting a sound like that of a mechanical toy being wound up, and run off like tiny ships under full sail. Stopped, they might about-face, hiss some more, and take off in another direction.

CHIMNEY SWIFT *(Chaetura pelagica)*

Sometimes I marvel at how frequently I have enjoyed watching Chimney Swifts in the sky and how very infrequently I have seen them anywhere else. No wonder the ancient Greeks, who never saw swifts alighting anywhere, thought that the birds had no feet!

Anyone who has handled a live Chimney Swift will never forget its feet. The toes are strong and the claws sharp and the feet have an almost comical way of grasping at anything within reach. Late one evening at the university's biological station in south-central Oklahoma my students and I banded a considerable number of swifts that were roosting in an old well. The birds entered the well through gaps between planks put there to keep people from falling in. After dark we removed the planks, surrounded the opening, held a big net over all of us umbrellawise, and dangled a nail on a string down into the well to stir the birds up. When the nail reached the uppermost birds we heard the roar of wings—a vaguely ominous sound, like that of an explosion. Down the nail went a bit farther and there was another muffled explosion. Then *whoof* came the exodus, and we were fairly smothered by swifts. Determined to get away, the birds continued to beat their wings whether clinging to something or not. The stiff tips of their tail feathers and their sharp claws dug into our skin. Many a bird alighted on a face, clawing at nose, lip, or eyebrow for a foothold. Not many birds got away without having an official band attached to one leg. Several that were banded that night were found nesting in other old wells of the neighborhood years afterwards.

A Chimney Swift's nest is a little basket of twigs stuck together with the bird's own saliva and fastened with the same cement to the inside of a chimney, well, or hollow tree. Sometimes it is fastened to the wall of a garage, barn, or deserted house. The gathering of twigs is well worth watching. The bird's feet are designed for clinging, not for walking or jumping, so gathering twigs is, like almost every other activity in a swift's life, aerial. Having found a dead or partly dead branch, the swift flies to it, snaps a section of slender twig off with its feet while flying, covers this with saliva either while flying or after it reaches the nest site, and adds it to the nest. The whole structure is not very big, but it takes many a twig to complete it. Both birds of the pair gather twigs. The glands that furnish the saliva are extraordinarily large at nest-building time.

Egg-laying starts before the nest is finished. The three to five pure white eggs are somewhat capsule-shaped. Both sexes incubate. The young hatch naked, but blood-quills soon appear and presently these feather-out at the tips. The brood now overcrowds the nest, so they climb out. Clinging with their strong toes, and using their stubby, spine-tipped tails as props, they huddle under the nest, there to await the return of a parent.

RUBY-THROATED HUMMINGBIRD *(Archilochus colubris)*

This, the only species of hummingbird found in eastern North America, migrates through and breeds in eastern Oklahoma. It has been seen westward almost to the Panhandle, but the hummingbird that breeds from central Oklahoma westward may well be the closely related Black-chinned species *(A. alexandri)*. Adult male Black-chins are dull black on the chin and upper throat and shining purple on the lower throat. Female Black-chins are indistinguishable from female Ruby-throats in the field.

Do not follow a male Ruby-throat hoping that he will lead you to a nest. He knows nothing about the nest. The female with whom he consorted earlier in the season has selected a nest site and built a nest quite on her own. She may have seen him occasionally, perhaps even fed from the same flowers that he has visited, but so independent of each other have the two become that the male now fiercely drives all females from his feeding spots, and, by the same token, if he happens to wander near a nest, the female at that nest drives him off no matter whose mate he is.

If you carefully watch a *female* Ruby-throat, she may lead you to the nest. If a hummer attacks you in the woods, really gets after you that is, buzzing in front of your face and making sharp, squeaky noises, the bird will almost certainly be a female. If, indeed, it is a female (throat light gray), sit right down and watch. Now that you have become less tall than you were, the hummer may go straight to her nest. She will be very matter-of-fact about the nest, her duties there, and you. Hardly does she reach the nest before she's in it, looking down at you.

More than one Ruby-throat's nest I have found by following through the woods the line of flight that a female bird has taken from a favorite feeding spot. The feeding spot may be a bed of flowering jewelweed, lobelia, or bee-balm. At our home in West Virginia we continued to see a female hummer in the yard day after day in May and early June, never dreaming that the little bird had a nest there. One afternoon we chanced to see her fly from honeysuckle flowers straight to her nest on an elm branch not more than 5 feet above the front walk. We had been using that walk, passing directly under the nest, for weeks. The two young hummers there were almost old enough to fly.

The nest is a beautiful little cup about the size of a walnut, softly lined with plant down and covered with lichens held in place with spider webbing. The two eggs are pure white. Only one brood is reared per season.

Adult male Ruby-throats are not often seen in Oklahoma in late summer and fall. Perhaps they leave for the south before the females and young do. Young birds of both sexes are much like the adult female, though young males are streaked with dark gray on the throat.

Courtesy Field Enterprises Educational Corporation.

23

COMMON FLICKER *(Colaptes auratus)*

This handsome bird is found throughout Oklahoma, but it is far commoner in winter than in summer. Both "yellow-shafted" and "red-shafted" forms breed here, the former chiefly in the northern half of the state, the latter only at the western end of the Panhandle. Yellow-shafted birds have much yellow on the major wing and tail feathers, a bright red patch on the nape, and (males only) a black malar stripe on each side of the face. Red-shafted birds have pinkish-red wing and tail linings, no red patch on the nape, and (males only) red malar stripes.

Flickers are woodpeckers, but they often alight perching-bird fashion on a dead branch at the top of a tree and sit there with tail hanging straight down; and they spend much time on the ground where they have no need to use the tail as a prop. On the ground they are usually after ants. Their extensile tongue, covered with sticky saliva, is designed for catching these insects. Flickers flushed from the ground in winter usually have found a sun-warmed ant-hill where that long tongue of theirs does its important work. Flickers often eat one surprising food item in winter—the berries of poison ivy.

The flicker's white rump-patch is noticeable when the bird flies up from the ground. The yellow or red of the wings usually flashes, too, so the species is not hard to identify. The word *flicker* may allude to the flashing or flickering of bright colors, but it also is a fair imitation of one of the bird's many call notes. The sharp *plee-kah*, a characteristic call, might also be written *flee-kah* or *flick-er*.

This call note usually accompanies "dancing," a frenzied prancing about with tail spread wide and head bobbing, behavior that looks as if it should be related to courtship, but that may be observed at any season and that sometimes involves three or more birds of the same sex. The ardor and seeming pointlessness of it all can be downright amusing.

Flickers nest in holes that they dig in trees. Since the entrance to the nest is just right for Starlings, the flickers have a running battle with the Starlings. In Norman the flicker has almost disappeared as a nesting bird because of the Starling. I did not realize how critical the situation had become until one day a few years ago when I heard a flicker shrieking from the ground just across the street from my house. Going to the rescue, I found a flicker on its back with wings spread, and on it a Starling that had been striking it savagely. Had I not intervened, I believe the Starling would have killed the flicker.

Flicker eggs are white and glossy. Six to eight are laid. Both sexes incubate. The young hatch naked but are well feathered by the time they leave the nest. Toward the end of the fledging period they crowd the entrance to the nest-hole, calling lustily when a parent returns.

Courtesy Field Enterprises Educational Corporation.

25

RED-BELLIED WOODPECKER *(Melanerpes carolinus)*

The Redbelly is often called the Red-headed Woodpecker, but that's a mistake. The Redbelly's head is scarlet above and gray below, whereas in the true Redhead the head is red all over and the shade is carmine or crimson. The true Redhead has a big white patch in the wing, too, a mark that shows plainly, especially when the bird flies. Another difference: male and female Redheads are colored alike, whereas in the female Redbelly the front half of the crown is gray, not red.

"Chiv" is my nickname for the Redbelly. *Chiv, chiv*, it cries from high in a tree, largely hidden behind a big branch. Not far away a squirrel barks and I, not being in a very scientific frame of mind, wonder whether the woodpecker learned its *chiv* from the squirrel or vice versa. Now the woodpecker, convinced that I am too close, flies to another tree and faces me, giving me a look at its underparts. Gray are its throat, foreneck, and chest. For the red of its belly I look in vain. That vague color shows with a specimen in hand, but it's of no use as a field mark.

The Redbelly is very fond of small fruits. It dotes on ripe mulberries. It also likes cherries, and I have watched it carrying sand plums, soapberries, and pokeberries to almost-fledged young in the nest. It is not the confirmed catcher of flying cicadas that the Redhead is, nor does it, so far as I know, cache food as that species does.

In spring the Redbelly becomes both drummer and songster. Now the male, clinging to a stub in which a nest cavity will presently be dug, calls *creer* in a voice that on a windless day sounds peaceful and dreamy, if not downright lazy. Gone is the urge to hunt for food, to display, to chase off rival males. The urge is to sing. Or perhaps to drum a bit. When nest-digging starts, both male and female work and singing may stop for a while, though it resumes when egg-laying begins.

The season of nest-building is not always idyllic, for about the time the cavity is half done, the Starlings arrive. This I know, for Redbellies have repeatedly tried to nest in an old maple tree near my house in Norman. Never have the Redbellies reared young there, despite my attempts to help them. In late April of 1959 I watched the birds at work day after day, for their nest was only about 12 feet up and in plain sight from my front porch. The Starlings did not come until the nest was well started; but the entrance was just right for them and once they found they could enter, the fighting started. I wanted to keep the woodpeckers, so started killing the Starlings. I killed several. Finally the woodpecker eggs were laid and I assumed that the Starlings had left. Alas, on my return from a weekend out of town, I found a Starling nest in the cavity and the woodpecker eggs were gone.

Courtesy the Carnegie Museum of Natural History.

27

YELLOW-BELLIED SAPSUCKER *(Sphyrapicus varius)*

This woodpecker drills rows of holes in the bark, lets sap gather in the holes and drinks the sap, which it shares with insects. The insects pay a stiff price for what they drink, for the sapsucker eats them, thus balancing its diet. A big cedar of Lebanon near my house has sapsucker wells all over its trunk and larger branches. Long white lines of dried pitch lead down from the wells. From my kitchen window I can watch a sapsucker as it drills new holes. The bird takes a comfortable position and proceeds to drill from one to four or five holes in a horizontal row without moving any part of its body much except for the head and neck.

If sap-wells girdle a young tree, the tree may die. People know this, so they call for help. I have the proper permits for collecting scientific specimens, so proceed to collect the offending sapsuckers. Some of them are exceedingly fat. A sizeable sapsucker population can be a real problem at a nursery. At a country place east of Norman, on March 9, 1957, I collected three sapsuckers that had been girdling and killing little pines.

Not all of what they drink is good for the sapsuckers. The statement applies chiefly to the sap of the sweet or black birch *(Betula lenta)*, a tree not found in Oklahoma. Sapsuckers seem to be overly fond of this tree's sap, which sometimes ferments a bit. With a bit of over-drinking, the sapsuckers become tipsy, occasionally so much so that they zigzag through the woods, bumping into trunks and branches. The facial expression of an incontinent sapsucker can be a trifle amusing, for it seems to declare that nothing's really wrong. Sapsuckers doubtless drink the sap of the river or red birch *(B. nigra)*, a tree that does grow in eastern Oklahoma, but I have never observed a "tipsy" sapsucker among our river birches.

Sapsuckers visit Oklahoma only during migration and in winter. They arrive from the north in late September and stay until about the last week of April (exceptionally to mid-May). They often find ornamental trees to their liking in towns. They are especially fond of the sap of conifers, fruit trees, and maples. Occasionally I have found their sap-wells in oaks and willows. They often eat the ripe fruits of the false buckthorn or chittamwood tree *(Bumelia lanuginosa)*.

A striking field mark is the big white patch in the wing. Young birds have an oddly speckled look during their first winter, a mixture of black, yellowish white, brown, and red, but the white wing-patch is always there. Adult males are rich red on the crown and throat, adult females red (sometimes more or less black) on the crown, and white on the throat. A characteristic call note is a sort of *mew,* not at all the sort of sound one might expect from a woodpecker.

Courtesy the Carnegie Museum of Natural History.

29

HAIRY WOODPECKER *(Picoides villosus)*

Be not content with calling the Hairy Woodpecker a "big edition" of the Downy. To be sure, each species is equipped with chisel-like bill, extensile, barb-tipped tongue, hyoid horns that lead from the tongue's base up over the skull and forward an unbelievable distance—in short, *le tout ensemble* of bones, muscles, and nerves of head and neck designed to withstand the terrific pecking, pounding, drilling, and prying required of an adult woodpecker every day of its existence. To be sure, the two species have about the same black-and-white plumage pattern, a slight difference being that in the Hairy the outer tail feathers are unmarked white, whereas in the Downy they are more or less barred with black. But in "personality" the two species are very unlike. The Downy is a confiding, somewhat meek little bird, the Hairy a bit wild-eyed and rambunctious.

In wooded parts of the United States and Canada the Hairy and the Downy live side by side. Throughout this vast area the Hairy is the larger. Indeed, the Hairies of the northwestern part of the continent are almost as large as flickers, whereas the Downies of that area are only about half that size. South of the United States, beyond the range of the Downy, the Hairy is a not very large montane bird found on wooded slopes.

In Oklahoma the Hairy is less common than the Downy, but both are to be looked for in all wooded areas, even in towns. The Hairy's hunting ground appears at first glance to be the same as that of the Downy, but actually it is different, for it is the trunks and larger branches, whereas the Downy seems to prefer the smaller branches and twigs, not to mention coarse, tall forbs such as giant ragweed, wild sunflower, and mullein—plants on which the Hairy rarely forages.

One Hairy nest that I visited daily some years ago was in a residential part of Norman in a slender, almost vertical dead cottonwood stub about 15 feet up. When I first saw it, on March 27, 1953, I was not sure who owned it, for two Carolina Chickadees were fighting noisily with the woodpeckers. The woodpeckers finally won out, the chickadees withdrew, and I was surprised to find that the male and female woodpecker, each of which incubated the eggs, behaved very differently at the nest. The female, roused by my "squeaking," would pop out promptly and fly off calling excitedly, or stick her head out, look about as if alarmed, then back in, whereas the male, when *he* was there, would "stay put," as if confident that my "squeaking" was not the real thing and therefore not worth investigating; even sharp rapping at the tree's base would not make him leave the eggs.

Courtesy the Carnegie Museum of Natural History.

31

DOWNY WOODPECKER *(Picoides pubescens)*

Bird music that I especially enjoy is the Downy Woodpecker's late winter drumming. Quite a percussionist is the Downy. How the little bird came to find that rapping on a dead stub could produce a worthwhile sound is hard to say. At any rate, drumming is today part of the Downy's time-honored way of laying claim to a territory; of announcing that a good spot for nesting has been found; of advising other Downies to find spots of their own and stay there.

The drumming starts quite a while before the warmth of spring is assured. A good drumming day need not be comfortable; indeed, its chilliness is sometimes sharp. But the sun is out part of the time and a persuasive syndrome of whistled chickadee calls, swelling buds, and patches of bright sky bespeaks the imminence of winter's passing.

Many a time I have watched a Downy drum-hunting. Less interested in food than in music, the bird flies from stub to stub, tapping here, tapping there, listening intently, eventually settling down where one tap promises what the Downy has in mind. There the bird stays, at this one very special spot, performing about every two minutes; and to this spot it returns. I listen closely, for on a good drumming day other Downies are likely to be at *their* drums. Sure enough, I hear another, perhaps a hundred yards away, and I wonder whether that one is a rival male or a female drummer, perhaps my drummer's mate.

The drumming is not in any way vocal. The usual vocal performance, a sharp *pick* or *peek*, indicates curiosity, perhaps suspicion, perhaps mere awareness of self. Given frequently when the nest is threatened by a squirrel, snake, or human being, it can become downright strident. Downy's song, if that be the right word for it, is a rattled-off series of these *peeks* given as a kind of declaration that all is well, often just before flight from high in a tree off through the woods.

The Downy's nest is a pecked-out cavity in a dead stub, with entrance too small for a Starling and with room 10 or 12 inches down for three to five chicks. The chicks are featherless at hatching, but by the time they are old enough to stick their heads out while calling for food, they look for all the world like their parents except for one important difference: the feathers of the top of the head are not black but are tipped with delicate pinkish-red in the males, with white in the females. Believers in the much-discussed theory of evolution point to this as proof that the Downy's male ancestors, long long ago, were red all over the crown rather than merely on the nape. I do not argue over matters of this sort, though the phrase "ontogeny repeats phylogeny" does sound impressive.

Perhaps I am too busy listening for that Downy drummer of mine, off among the trees. He is a "different drummer," all right, and well worth listening to. Henry David Thoreau please take note.

Courtesy the Carnegie Museum of Natural History.

EASTERN KINGBIRD *(Tyrannus tyrannus)*

Known as the "Bee Martin" in many parts of the United States, this tyrant flycatcher does not feed on honey bees, though it has been observed to catch them; and of course it is not a martin, for martins belong to the swallow family. *Kingbird* is a good name, because the bird has a regal way of chasing birds of prey, and because it wears a gorgeous "crown" of orange-scarlet that is concealed most of the time under the black plumage of the top of its head.

I recall only one occasion on which I clearly saw this crown-patch in a wild, free-flying bird. I had been told of a nest containing almost fledged young in a sycamore close to a certain pond. "You can't miss it," my informant had said. But miss it I did until I chanced to see one of the young birds fluttering from some leaves that hid the nest to a bare stretch of the supporting branch. At that same instant one of the parent birds quit its excited outcry and headed straight for me rapidly, silently. When it was about ten feet away its crown-patch suddenly flared, its mandibles snapped loudly, and for one instant of shock I felt as if a firecracker had exploded near my face.

Tyrannus tyrannus is famous for its intrepid chasing of hawks and crows or, for that matter, of any "big bad bird." A beleaguered Turkey Vulture can be downright comical, for the wide-winged vulture is incapable of doing anything but gliding stolidly, ponderously on. No matter how flustered its psyche may be, it seems to realize that flapping its wings will not help a bit, that attempting to turn quickly will only waste energy, that grinning and bearing is about all it can do. A large hawk moving above orchards or open woods "owned" by kingbirds knows no peace, for one pair of kingbirds drives it to the limits of their home range, at which point another pair of kingbirds promptly takes over.

What a person usually sees of an Eastern Kingbird in the field is the clear white of its underparts and the darkness of its upperparts. Its whole tail is tipped with white—a reliable field mark. Males and females are alike. Their usual cry, which may be written *pi-tink*, is usually repeated several times.

Tyrannus tyrannus breeds widely in Oklahoma, though it is decidedly uncommon in summer in the southwestern part of the state. In the Black Mesa country it is much less common than the Western Kingbird *(T. verticalis)*. On the university campus in Norman, where several pairs of Western Kingbirds have nested regularly during the past twenty-odd years, I have never found more than one pair of Eastern Kingbirds. This pair has nested close to the "duck pond," as a rule on a branch overhanging the water. The *Western* Kingbird usually nests well away from water.

ge Miksch Sutton

Courtesy the Carnegie Museum of Natural History.

WESTERN KINGBIRD *(Tyrannus verticalis)*

This bird of scattered woods, open pastureland, parks, and campuses is a confirmed lover of hot weather. When it arrives in spring—usually in mid-April—I know that winter is over. On chilly, drizzly days it looks miserable. Indeed, I know of no sorrier sight in the bird world than a wet Western Kingbird.

The species is common locally in western Oklahoma, the eastern limits of its breeding being as a rule in the vicinity of Tulsa, Oklahoma City, Norman, and Ardmore. The Eastern Kingbird breeds throughout the whole state, so western Oklahoma is an area of overlap. In Texas County, in the Panhandle, I found a pair of Western Kingbirds and a pair of Eastern Kingbirds nesting in the same large cottonwood tree near Coldwater Creek. The pairs had settled their arguments by the time I found them, but I noticed that they had built their nests as far apart as possible without descending to sand plum thickets close by.

Along the Cimarron River in the Black Mesa country of Cimarron County the Western Kingbird is one of the commonest summer birds. When it arrives there from the south it is also one of the noisiest. Until pairs have formed and territories have been established, there is constant bickering throughout the daylight hours. After nests have been built and eggs laid, things settle down a bit, but the hubbub resumes when danger threatens.

Nests are usually in an exposed place on a horizontal branch. Whenever I see a Western Kingbird alighting on the ground and pulling at grass-roots, I know that a nest is being built. Twine is often used, too. Twice during the past twenty-some years I have rescued birds that have become entangled by twine, and on another occasion someone brought me a dead one that he had found dangling from the nest-tree. So far as I know, only the female builds the nest. Some nests are placed on crossbars of telephone poles or on TV antennas. The hotter the spot the better, it would seem.

In Norman, several pairs of Western Kingbirds have nested every summer on and near the university campus. As a rule the nests have been in Chinese elms on branches that were dead or partly dead. As the Chinese elms have died and been removed, the kingbirds have nested in American elms, sycamores, and pines. A pair that has nested regularly near the Stovall Museum has brought its brood summer after summer to a wire that hangs between the main building and the next building to the south. The young ones are a pretty sight, lined up in a row, all headed in the same direction. They are not yet old enough to catch their own food. It recently dawned on me why this spot is so popular. The old birds find food galore each morning on the ground, the shrubbery, and the sides of the buildings near lights that have attracted insects during the night.

SCISSOR-TAILED FLYCATCHER *(Muscivora forficata)*

The Scissortail, Oklahoma's state bird, is among the world's most beautiful feathered creatures. The soft pale gray of its head and back is the perfect foil for the lovely salmon-pink of its underparts, as well as for the black parts of its long, deeply forked tail. Perched on a wire or dead branch, it holds its tail horizontally. A bit of bright color rarely seen is the scarlet-vermilion of its crown-patch, a feature found in adult males and some first-year males but not, so far as I know, in females. In first-year males the tail is longer than that of adult females, but shorter than that of adult males.

The beauty of the Scissortail is greatest not in spring and summer but in fall, just before departure for the south. Now great numbers of adult and young birds roost together while completing the molt. Roost-trees are sometimes in a residential part of town. To them the birds come by the score in late afternoon and evening. In the morning, as they all scatter for the day, some males fly upward, twittering and tumbling about as if in courtship display. The call that accompanies these performances is a spirited *pit, pit, pit-a-whit*, repeated over and over. The same call is given in the predawn twilight during the breeding season by the male bird perched in the top of a tree not far from the nest.

Scissortails are not forest birds; they like a scattering of trees. Their nests are, like those of the Western Kingbird, often placed in an exposed position—even on the crossbar of a telephone pole. The female does the building, though the male often accompanies her as she gathers material. A clutch of four or five eggs is the rule, and two broods are sometimes reared in a season. This I discovered during the summer of 1954 when, at the University of Oklahoma Biological Station, my class and I visited daily a low nest in a persimmon sapling. We marked the eggs, banded the young ones, were scolded by the old birds, eventually witnessed the fledging. Not expecting to obtain proof of two-broodedness, I chanced to visit the nest one evening a week or so later and to my surprise found the female sitting in it, surrounded by her first brood. The banded young ones had fairly long tails by that time and pretty they were as they formed a circle, each within inches of its mother. Four eggs were in the nest.

The Scissortail breeds widely in Oklahoma westward to the 100th meridian. In heavily wooded parts of the state it nests chiefly along highways. In the Panhandle scattered pairs breed as far west as Guymon. In Cimarron County the species is decidedly uncommon at all seasons.

Courtesy the University of Oklahoma Foundation.

EASTERN PHOEBE *(Sayornis phoebe)*

The Eastern Phoebe has an important place in the history of the bird-banding movement, for Audubon himself caught a nesting pair of the little birds in a "grotto" along Perkiomen Creek near Philadelphia in the spring of 1804, tied a silver thread on one leg of each, and two years later saw the thread on one of the pair that were nesting in the same cavern.

Sayornis phoebe is grayish olive above, darker on the head than on the back, and yellowish white below. It has no wingbars. It wags its tail frequently, not from side to side but up and down. Its *fit-a-bee* and *zhee-bee* callnotes are gentle. A hardy bird, it often winters in Oklahoma, especially in the southeastern part of the state. It feeds largely on insects caught midair, hence it winters where water usually remains unfrozen, some aquatic vegetation remains green, and such insects as midges, mosquitoes, craneflies, and moths move about during warm hours of the day.

Eastern Phoebes that winter south of Oklahoma return in early spring, often to the very bridges or culverts at which they have nested for years. Nests built on metal girders, wooden planks, or projecting stones may remain in place and be used again, but nests attached to vertical walls without support directly below them sometimes fall. At Norman, phoebes nest in a small cement-lined culvert near Hospital Lake almost every year. Often the pair rears two broods in a season. The nest is attached to the wall just far enough from the culvert's top to permit the phoebe to slip in and out. How the nest manages to cling there has mystified me, for it has no obvious support. This past season it was built afresh and eggs were laid, but it fell, perhaps when a female cowbird visited it, and the phoebes left the culvert.

The eggs, which number 4 to 6, are white, sometimes immaculate, but usually marked with widely scattered dark spots. Young phoebes remain in the nest for sixteen or seventeen days. They are able to fly fairly well when they leave. Fledging is fraught with dangers, for the nest is often over water and the young bird's first flight may be unsuccessful. A friend of mine who banded a brood only a day or so before they were ready to leave watched one of the little birds flutter from the nest just after he had attached a band to its leg. The nest was under a bridge above fairly deep water. The nestling flew fairly well and did not fall into the water; but it barely reached the shore, several yards away, where it was promptly caught by a frog that would surely have gulped it down had not my friend gone to the rescue.

Eastern though *Sayornis phoebe* is, it breeds westward throughout Oklahoma. Where there are no bridges, culverts, or cliffs, it nests in barns or deserted houses.

Courtesy the Carnegie Museum of Natural History.

41

ROUGH-WINGED SWALLOW *(Stelgidopteryx ruficollis)*

Some years ago, along a dry streambed leading northward from Lake Texoma, I found several pairs of Rough-winged Swallows nesting close to each other in burrows in vertical parts of the high earthen banks. Most of the nests were close enough to the bottom of the gully for me to reach my arm in without a ladder. The burrows, which seemed overlarge for so small a bird, led back horizontally, most of them so far that the nests were beyond reach. Two nests that I did reach (14 inches or so back) were composed of dry grass, weed-stems, leaves, and little pods. There were no feathers. The date was too late for eggs; the several young that I handled were well feathered, but not yet ready to fly.

The entrances to the burrows were well apart and out of sight of each other. It was as if the birds did not want to be reminded of each other, this despite the fact that they occasionally lined up sociably on telephone wires not far away. As the old birds came and went they flew so close to the bottom of the gully that when I approached at pasture-level I never saw them. Most puzzling of all was the absence of evidence that the swallows had dug the burrows. Below the entrances I could not find the slightest pile of loose earth. What, then, had dug them? As I examined the entrances carefully, I decided that the birds themselves had done the digging, carrying off each mouthful and spitting it out so far away that it could not possibly lead some predator to the nest. Certainly the birds' instincts were powerful: at not one burrow could even the largest of snakes have managed to get in, for the several-foot stretch of wall above and below the entrance was sheer and vertical.

When I brought the young swallows out for a look, they clung to my fingers with their strong toes. Never before had they seen so much daylight. The total impact of man, gully, and sky must have been overwhelming. I could not help wondering what those little eyes were actually seeing, what went on in the little brains. This much I do know: when put back into their tunnel those nestlings scuttled toward the spot they knew about. They made no attempt to prove to the world that they were ready to conquer it.

The Roughwing is the least colorful of Oklahoma's swallows. It is earthy brown above, light gray on the throat and breast, white on the belly and under tail coverts. It differs from the Bank Swallow *(Riparia riparia)* in having no dark brown band across the chest. Its name is derived from the actual roughness of the outer web of its outermost primary wing feather, a roughness that can be detected by running a fingernail along it.

George Miksch Sutton

Courtesy the Carnegie Museum of Natural History.

BARN SWALLOW *(Hirundo rustica)*

Northwest of Norman, near the airfield, is a shallow impoundment that I have always called the Airfield Pond. When there are heavy rains this pond overflows, covering an acre or so of old pavement with water up to an inch or so deep, but often it shrinks to a mere puddle at the west end, leaving a big, slightly muddy flat that dries up quickly. Near the pond, on scattered occasions in late summer, I have witnessed a phenomenon that I have never been able to explain—the gathering of hundreds of Barn Swallows, young birds and old, so thickly massed on the hot pavement that at a distance they look like a big black blot. Using a binocular, I have done my best to decide why the birds were there. Under them was no dust in which they might have bathed. Not one of them made a move toward the water's edge for a drink or bath. So far as I could see, no midges or insects of other sorts were flying above the water. Some birds preened a bit or lifted wings for a stretch, but most of the time all of them merely sat, as if resting.

On the afternoon of August 29, 1961, I put such a flock to flight. A pretty sight they were as they crossed and recrossed the wettish place in which the pond had been. A few skimmed a drink from water at the west end, but, so far as I could see, not one of the flock left the area. Within a few minutes the entire company was back where it had been, most of them on the ground, a few perched on low weeds. There were no telephone wires thereabouts, but the birds spurned a fence that crossed the pond's west end. For some reason they preferred the ground. Could they have been attracted by insects that they had eaten before settling down? Were they benefiting in some way from the heat of the pavement? No such behavior have I observed in other parts of the species' really vast breeding range.

Oklahoma's Barn Swallows are decidedly colonial. In West Virginia, New York, Pennsylvania, and Michigan, where I have seen much of the species, pairs have seemed to prefer nesting separately. Where two pairs have nested in the same barn, the pairs have chosen separate parts of the building, coming and going through different doors or windows. But in Oklahoma's big culverts Barn Swallows nest in considerable numbers within inches of each other, sometimes even in company with Cliff Swallows *(Petrochelidon pyrrhonota)*, a notable difference between the species being that Cliff Swallow nests often touch each other or even overlap, whereas Barn Swallow nests are virtually always at least an inch or so apart from one another.

PURPLE MARTIN *(Progne subis)*

This well-known, much loved bird is the largest of our swallows. Males are shiny purplish black; females gray, darker above than below, with bluish shine in dark parts of the plumage; first-year males much like females. First-year males are believed to breed. They are part of almost every large breeding colony.

The species is highly colonial, separate nesting pairs being the exception. One such pair built a nest in a broken traffic light at a major street intersection in Gate, at the eastern end of the Panhandle, but no one knows whether eggs were laid in that nest. At the University of Oklahoma Biological Station, on the north shore of Lake Texoma, a large colony has flourished for years, nesting in several houses, all of them placed well away from trees. At this colony mortality has been high chiefly because young birds crawl from the nests and fall to the ground long before fledging. What leads the nestlings to do this has puzzled everyone summer after summer.

The Purple Martin is one-brooded. Four to six white eggs are laid. Only the female incubates, the incubation period lasting fifteen or sixteen days. Fledging requires a little less than a month. During the latter part of the fledging period, the young are fed many dragonflies. What I now have to say about this important fact may strike some birdlovers as sheer heresy.

Martins are alleged to be great mosquito eaters. So widely held is this belief that communities go to great lengths to attract martins, putting up expensive houses for them, organizing drives against House Sparrows and Starlings, etc. In my carefully considered opinion, martins have little to do with controlling mosquitoes. Most mosquitoes do not fly about much on bright days and when they do fly they keep to shadowy places that martins do not visit. Martins must surely catch some mosquitoes along with gnats, midges, craneflies, and the like, but the mosquitoes just happen to be caught. Expending much energy on capturing such small fry would be poor economy. Martins and their progeny need something more substantial. One insect to which they often turn is the dragonfly, a creature that *does* eat mosquitoes. The martin that eats one dragonfly may, in a sense, be saving the lives of scores, perhaps hundreds, of mosquitoes. The fact that martins eat dragonflies will be evident to anyone who watches carefully the incoming parent birds, for the wings of the dragonflies are clearly visible at each side of the bill.

Do not misunderstand me. I, too, love martins. I think their *putt, putt, putt* and *ee-bird* cries are among the jolliest sounds in nature. But I do not love the birds for any fancied value they may have as controllers of mosquitoes.

47

BLUE JAY *(Cyanocitta cristata)*

Anyone who says he hates Blue Jays interests me. Such a person tells me of "one of those big bullies" that drives the little birds from a feeding counter, then fills its gullet with expensive sunflower seeds. I comment that the jay may not be eating the seeds but merely carrying them off to spots known only to itself. "It's a way jays have," I explain. This confirms the jay hater's belief and lessens his hatred a little, for in me he has found a comrade-in-arms, so he goes on to tell me of the robbing of a robin's nest: "That scoundrel took every egg in spite of all the racket the old robins made."

I now describe in detail the robbing of a dove's nest. "I had just got down from the willow I had climbed to see whether the dove's eggs were fresh. While I was standing to one side, more or less hidden, a jay flew over. It must not have seen me, but it did see the two white dove eggs, so down it wheeled, straight to the nest. Perhaps I should have shooed it off, but I didn't, for I was fascinated by its behavior. Right in front of me it ate the two eggs and flew off."

Thus does the seminar continue, for each of us has tales to tell. One of mine is about the jay that pecked me on the forehead when I, a mere kid, was stealing one of its babies from a nest. "That bird bored a hole in me. The blood ran down all over my face!" My friend recalls Mark Twain's wonderful yarn about the jay that put acorns into a hole in the roof, figuring that they'd taste good come winter, but never quite filling up the hole. "And say," continues my companion, "have you ever seen a jay standing high on its legs and bobbing all over while it makes that funny *pee-deedle* sound?" There's a moment's silence. "That reminds me," I respond. "I had a class looking into a tree at the north end of Canton Reservoir one day, trying to see a Screech Owl that was trilling as those little owls do. We looked and looked, but couldn't see a thing, though we completely surrounded the tree and the trilling continued right above us. Then the trilling stopped and out flew the jay, squawking as if laughing its head off."

Seriously now, the Blue Jay is one of Oklahoma's most successful birds, biologically speaking. It inhabits woodland westward to the New Mexico line, often being common in towns, especially in winter. It is regularly two-brooded. Many first nests for the season are started in late March, and first broods are out about six weeks later.

One final blow: the blue of a Blue Jay's plumage is not pigmentary. It is a structural color, the result of a breaking up of light rays by minute parts of the feathers—another way of saying, it would seem, that a Blue Jay is not really blue at all. It merely looks that way.

CAROLINA CHICKADEE *(Parus carolinensis)*

The Carolina Chickadee is non-migratory, but it gives the impression of being with us only in winter because it visits feeding counters so frequently at that season and is seen so little otherwise. In spring, once the nest is built and the eggs are laid, the pair becomes secretive. Now the female spends much of her time on the eggs, the male regularly feeds her while she is on the nest, and the two of them roam the woods together only for short spells during which the female gets a bit of exercise and finds some food on her own.

The nest is in a cavity, often an old woodpecker hole. It is made of moss, hair, and other soft materials. Both birds build it and building starts early. On February 21, 1954 I watched a pair carrying plant down to an old woodpecker hole on the university campus, but I obtained no proof that young were reared there. Successful nesting usually starts in April. The eggs, which are white, speckled with reddish brown, number five to seven, sometimes more. The incubating bird sits very close. At many a nest I have tapped the stub or post, failed to frighten the bird off, and decided that the eggs were deserted; yet when I investigated further I found that the little bird had been there all the while.

If she leaves because of the intrusion, she summons her mate with a spirited *chick-a-dee-dee-dee-dee*. Together they give this call excitedly, continuing the outcry until all the birds of the neighborhood have gathered. When we withdraw, the hubbub dies down, the female pops back into the nest-hole, and the male flies off.

So many photographs have been taken of young chickadees lined up on a twig that an incorrect concept of the fledging procedure has taken root. Actually the brood does not leave the nest until they are all fairly well developed. Comes the "moment of truth" and out they all pour, flying so well that we can't help wondering how much practicing has gone on inside the nest cavity. Now, keeping together, they troop through the woods foraging. The young ones are just like their parents save that their plumage is fresh and soft. The old birds by this time are a bit shop-worn, for they have been busy.

One brood is reared per season. The family often forms the nucleus of a small-bird flock that goes about as a sort of unit. Every seasoned bird student knows that in fall and winter a sure way to find birds is to listen for a chickadee. Where there's one chickadee there almost certainly will be others, not to mention a woodpecker or two, some Tufted Titmice *(Parus bicolor)*, perhaps a nuthatch, perhaps a Brown Creeper *(Certhia familiaris)*. Find the chickadee and you find them all!

Courtesy the Carnegie Museum of Natural History.

BEWICK'S WREN *(Thryomanes bewickii)*

Of the five wrens that breed regularly in Oklahoma, the Bewick's is the only one found all year throughout the whole state. It is less common in winter than in summer as a rule, so it may migrate to some extent. In treeless parts of the Panhandle it lives in towns, around farm buildings, and along brush-lined streambeds whether these have water in them or not. In northern Oklahoma it lives side-by-side in summer with the House Wren *(Troglodytes aedon)*, a species of similar size, habits, and habitat requirements. Both nest in cavities of various sorts, hence often in birdhouses. In some areas they compete—at times fiercely—for nest-sites. House Wrens have been known to puncture Bewick's Wren eggs in some areas of overlap, but this has not been observed in Oklahoma, so far as I know.

In color, the Bewick's differs from the House chiefly in having a white line above the eye and whiter underparts. Its tail is longer. The light gray marks at its tail corners are distinctive. Furthermore, the Bewick's has a characteristic way of spreading and wagging its tail, a custom that has led some observers to call the bird "loose-tailed"—a term they would not apply to the House Wren.

The songs of the two species are bright and hurried. That of the Bewick's nearly always ends with a well-defined trill, whereas the House Wren's bubbles on from phrase to phrase without a trill or pause anywhere. A strange little call of the Bewick's is a subdued *burb-burb*, a note that may indicate suspicion or curiosity. Its scold, like that of the House Wren, is harsh and rasping. According to my observations, the scold is reserved for times when the eggs or young are threatened.

Some Bewick's nests that I have observed in Oklahoma have been in surprising places. One was on the ground near a deserted house under an upside-down washtub, another in a rusted tin can on a shelf in a garage, another in a tractor parked in a shed. Nests are warmly lined with feathers, some of which curl upward and inward in such a way as to hide the cup and its contents. The four to six white eggs are speckled with brown at the larger end.

Only the female Bewick's Wren incubates the eggs. Two broods are reared. Broods stay together for some time after fledging, moving about as a flock. Often in late summer and fall I have noted that when I come upon one Bewick's Wren, I come upon several, and I suspect that these scattered companies are composed of parent birds and the two broods that they have reared.

Courtesy the Carnegie Museum of Natural History.

CAROLINA WREN *(Thryothorus ludovicianus)*

Wrens are small brown birds whose tails stick straight up much of the time. All but one of the sixty-some species in the wren family are found only in the New World. The one found in both worlds is known in the United States and Canada as the Winter Wren *(Troglodytes troglodytes)*, in England simply as the Wren. That very small species is found in Oklahoma only in winter.

A considerably larger species, one that is reddish brown above and buffy below, is the Carolina Wren, whose song calls to mind some such word as *teakettle*. The *teakettle* is repeated three or four times, rhythmically and merrily. If, while other birds are silent in the shady woods, the song explodes close by, it can be startling. At times the words *which jailer* catch the swing of the song better than *teakettle* does—another way of saying that songs vary from individual to individual; that what a bird sings may sound differently to different persons; or that a given bird may have song-phrases of two or more sorts. I know this last to be true, for a Carolina Wren that has been singing recently in my yard often switches from one phrase to another.

In Norman three wren species nest, the big Carolina and two smaller ones, the Bewick's and the House. Most House Wren nestings have been unsuccessful during the past twenty-some years. All three species have nested in my neighborhood, the Bewick's and House in birdboxes, the Carolina in a pile of wood stacked for the fireplace, in a potted plant hanging from a porch roof, on a shelf in a garage, or against a brick wall back of vines. The Carolina rarely uses a birdhouse, though I have observed a nest in one corner of a wooden crate under a house, another in a discarded refrigerator with door left ajar, another on a dresser top near an unscreened window left continuously open.

Away from town, the Carolina inhabits bottomland woods chiefly, nesting among exposed roots along streambanks and in holes on sloping ground among dead leaves. Nests are bulky—made of weedstalks, rootlets, dead grass, and leaf skeletons—and neatly domed-over. The eggs, which number four to six, are white, heavily speckled with reddish brown. The incubating bird sits so closely and comes and goes so secretively that nests are not often found. Those that we do find are usually discovered after the eggs have hatched. Now the old birds, carrying billfuls of insects and spiders, are not as cautious as they were while eggs were in the nest.

The Carolina Wren is common in wooded parts of eastern and central Oklahoma. Farther west it is found only in dense lowland woods close to the larger streams. It has been seen and heard as far west as Guymon in the Panhandle, but it is not known to have nested there. It is non-migratory.

Courtesy the Carnegie Museum of Natural History.

AMERICAN ROBIN *(Turdus migratorius)*

They may be "dog days" in other parts of the Northern Hemisphere when mid-August arrives, but in my back yard they're ragged robin days. The weather's hot and dry. The sprinkler's going full blast and so are the robins, old ones with plain red breasts, young ones with speckled breasts, all molting. I have to admit that they're not pretty. On one a great patch of belly feathers is missing—possibly clawed out by a cat; another is minus so many head feathers that a lot of basic robin shows; two have such boldly white tail-corners that I fetch the binocular: the white tip of the outermost feather on each side is noticeable since all the middle feathers, which usually cover the white tips, have dropped out.

Despite their frowziness, the robins are a sight to see. The sprinkler has brought angleworms to the surface, so off in one corner a tug of war is on. The worm is losing. Every robin shivers ecstatically when water hits it. Each leans forward now and then to sip from a tiny puddle in the grass. Each snatches and gulps down some item so small that I can't tell what it is. This bothers me. Here am I, a confirmed ornithologist, and there they are, everybody's dooryard birds, yet I can't tell what they're swallowing. For all I know, it may be several things—woodlice, half-drowned ants, butterfly eggs, what not.

One robin, fairly drenched, flies lazily up into the big cedar of Lebanon, shakes its plumage, and preens. There's nothing casual about the preening. Out drop feathers, one by one, two by two. For all the wetness at their tips, the feathers are partly dry, so down they float. Since the big tree is a favorite retreat for molting robins, there are lots of feathers under it. A good many droppings, too, though the robins don't roost there.

Nobody needs to be told much about robins. They have a charming habit of singing in the rain. Most singing, rain or shine, is from perches in trees, but now and then I see a robin singing from the ground. Whisper songs, *sotto voce*, are a delight to hear. An evening chorus of robin song brings the poet in me out. How the simple, homespun phrases interweave; what a fine fabric of sound they become!

I have never seen sky quite the blue of a robin's egg. But I must remember—and for this I am deeply grateful—that I still have sky to look at. Most robin nests hold three or four eggs. Only the female incubates. When the brood leaves the nest both parents feed them for several days. There's something heart-warming about the way in which a hungry young one follows the old bird about, getting fed, getting fed again, begging, getting fed some more, then looking at the wiggling piece of worm that's been put in front of it, picking this up, dropping it, picking it up again—and finally swallowing the by-this-time quiescent morsel without help from anyone.

SWAINSON'S THRUSH *(Catharus ustulatus)*

Two well-known Oklahoma birds, the American Robin and Eastern Bluebird, belong to the thrush family, though no one ever calls them thrushes. Of the several Oklahoma birds that are actually called thrushes, the only one that breeds here is the Wood Thrush *(Hylocichla mustelina)*, a fine songster found chiefly in the eastern third of the state. But the commonest thrush by far is the Swainson's, a transient. At the height of its migrations, this species is found throughout the state not only in woodlands but in residential parts of cities.

The Swainson's Thrush is olive-brown above, grayish white below, with not very heavy dark streaking on the chest and a buffy eye-ring. The eye-ring is distinctive. The species' closest relatives, the Gray-cheeked Thrush *(Catharus minimus)*, Veery *(C. fuscescens)*, and Hermit Thrush *(C. guttatus)*, all of which migrate through Oklahoma (the Hermit often winters, too) do not have it. The Gray-cheek looks very much like the Swainson's except that its whole face is gray; the Veery is much more reddish brown throughout its upper parts than either the Swainson's or the Gray-cheek; and the Hermit, which is woodsy brown above, has a more or less reddish brown tail that it lifts occasionally in a characteristic way. I say "more or less" here advisedly, for certain western races of the Hermit Thrush that pass through western Oklahoma and that winter there occasionally are *not* very reddish brown on the tail. These birds are gray enough on the face to look much like Gray-cheeked Thrushes. So identifying the Swainson's with certainty may not be nearly so difficult as being sure about some Hermit Thrushes that happen not to lift their tails while being watched. Gray-faced birds seen in early spring (before April 21) are likely to be Hermit Thrushes rather than Gray-cheeked thrushes.

As for songs, that of the Swainson's is the only one that spirals upward. Songs of the Veery and Gray-cheek both spiral downward. The Hermit's, which does not spiral in either direction, starts on a high note and continues with short notes that go both up and down. I have never heard the Hermit sing in Oklahoma. Songs of the Swainson's and Gray-cheek I hear every spring, sometimes right in my yard, but not in fall.

The Swainson's most characteristic callnote is a clearly enunciated *prrt* that reminds me of water dripping. This call I hear every spring, less often in fall. A characteristic call of the Gray-cheek (and also of the Veery) sounds like *view*. The Hermit gives a low *chook*.

Courtesy the Carnegie Museum of Natural History.

EASTERN BLUEBIRD *(Sialia sialis)*

Among the most exciting colors in the world is the blue of a flying male bluebird's back when it is seen from above on a bright day. For years my office on the campus was on the third floor of the Zoology Building. There, in winter, I often watched Eastern Bluebirds eating mistletoe berries in a treetop not far from the windows. When the birds had eaten their fill they became thirsty. Snow had melted in the street, so down to the puddles the bluebirds went. The color that I looked for did not show as they descended, but when they spread their wings and tail wide just before alighting, it flashed from the males as if lights had been turned on. It was intense, vibrant, unbelievable. I never saw it without marvelling. If I looked *up* at the same birds, I could see the reddish brown of their breasts and a hint of blue on their upperparts, but no blue comparable to what I have just described.

The female Eastern Bluebird is largely gray on her upperparts, though there is some blue on her wings and tail. Her breast is ruddy. The flecking or spotting of young birds is a character found throughout the Turdidae, the Thrush Family, to which all New World birds that are known as bluebirds belong.

Sialia sialis breeds northward to southern Canada in eastern North America and southward in the Rocky Mountain cordillera from southeastern Arizona to Nicaragua. It breeds throughout all of Oklahoma. A few pairs nest regularly along the Cimarron River in the Black Mesa country near Kenton. It winters irregularly in the state, chiefly in the eastern half.

Nests are in tree cavities, often old woodpecker holes. Nests in fenceposts are sometimes well away from the woods. Bluebirds like nestboxes, too. If these are placed in areas having an abundance of insect food, many pairs may nest fairly close to each other in a sort of colony. The nest itself is made largely of dry grass, without either feathers or hair in the lining. The female does all the building and it is she who incubates the four to six pale blue eggs.

Nesting starts early, and two broods are reared each season. I have never seen young of the first brood carrying food to nests containing unfledged young, but on several occasions I have seen adults and young of the first brood going about together while the old birds were carrying food to the nest, and I recall seeing, along the north shore of Lake Texoma, two molting parent birds accompanied by both of their broods. Young of the earlier brood had been out of the nest for some time and were in heavy molt. Young of the second brood, while well fledged and not dependent on their parents for food, were still in their full juvenal plumage.

George Miksch Sutton

Courtesy the Carnegie Museum of Natural History.

CEDAR WAXWING *(Bombycilla cedrorum)*

Now and then an ornithological experience can be shocking. One that came my way a few winters ago had to do with Cedar Waxwings. A woman who lived not far from me hailed me one day asking what the little birds were that she'd been seeing just outside her window. "The ends of their tails are yellow, light yellow," she said. Knowing that the only North American birds with yellow-tipped tails are waxwings, and that many Cedar Waxwings had recently been seen in town, I said with some assurance that her birds were Cedar Waxwings. Her reply was withering: "It doesn't matter what their name is. I wish you'd kill them. They've eaten all my berries." Never before had it occurred to me that berries might be more desirable than waxwings.

As a rule I hear nothing but praise for this bird, which is certainly among the loveliest of feathered beings to look at and among the most interesting to observe. The way it moves about in flocks is impressive. Twenty or thirty birds may be feeding together on hackberries. Suddenly one bird decides that a drink is in order, so down it flies to a fountain, the edge of a brook, or a puddle in the street. As it drinks it is joined by two more, then five or six more, then the rest of the flock. As they sip they crowd each other, but there is no sparring. Refreshed, they fly up, not to the berry supply (the berries may all be gone!) but to a leafless branch where they all sit as if half asleep until one of them decides that it's time to do something else.

Sometimes—alas, not infrequently—the flock does the wrong thing. Hastening to another feeding, drinking, or resting spot, the birds may fail to distinguish between the sky and a window's reflection of that sky, so into the glass they crash. Some are only stunned, but some die. Every autumn, waxwings are brought to me dead or almost dead about the time the species arrives for its winter sojourn here.

The sojourn may be short or long depending on the food supply. Favorite berries seem to be those of mistletoe and hackberry, but those of holly, Pyracantha, Virginia creeper, and privet all are consumed. Large holly bushes on the campus may be bright red with berries one day and utterly colorless the next, after the visit of a hundred or so waxwings.

Mistletoe berries, always swallowed whole, pass through the waxwing's alimentary tract without being thoroughly digested. The outer part of the seeds, the skin, is digested, but the seeds themselves, which have a thick, sticky covering, leave the body with the droppings, cling to twigs and dry there, waiting for a spring rain. Properly dampened, they germinate, new plants grow, seeds form on the mature plants, and a continuing food supply for waxwings is assured.

Courtesy the Carnegie Museum of Natural History.

63

LOGGERHEAD SHRIKE *(Lanius ludovicianus)*

Anyone who drives around Oklahoma much will see a not very large, somewhat bigheaded bird now and then perched on a telephone wire. It is gray above and white below, black-and-white on wings and tail, and black on the face. It sits horizontally, with tail sticking straight back. Put to flight, it drops to within a few feet of the ground, keeps at that level as it makes off in a straight line, and swoops up to another perch. Something like a Mockingbird in color, though not in behavior, it is a Loggerhead Shrike, a predatory songbird sometimes called the Butcher-bird.

The Loggerhead likes open country. In spring it is widely distributed in pairs, each pair with its deep, warmly lined nest in a bois d'arc or other thorny tree. In summer, family groups go about together, the young birds receiving food until they have learned to fend for themselves. But in winter each shrike leads a solitary life.

Anyone who watches the Loggerhead is in for surprises. Hook-billed though the bird is, it sings nicely in early spring. Some of its song phrases sound as if borrowed from other birds. The singing is not loud and it has a meditative quality, as if the bird might be practicing in private for public performance later.

Loggerheads consume animal food largely. When grasshoppers are common, these are eaten almost exclusively. Some are torn apart and swallowed on the spot, others impaled on thorns. Butchershops deserve close study. Often they contain mice, small birds, lizards, even snakes. One that I happened upon as a youngster in Texas was a stretch of barbed-wire fence to which a Loggerhead was attaching a giant water beetle. The insect was tough. The shrike could not get it stuck onto the barb. I moved up, finally almost within touching distance. The shrike did not fly off, but stayed with its prey, scolding me harshly. There was something exciting about being so close.

Banding Loggerheads caught in a mist-net can be painful for the bander, since the bird bites hard, often drawing blood. Though handled gently, petted, and talked to, it does not tame down. I am quite willing to let someone else band all adult Loggerheads. The young ones I can deal with.

One day my class and I saw a Loggerhead fly from one perch to a new one at the top of a small hawthorn. There the bird acted uncomfortable, twisting and shaking its head. Presently up and out came a pellet, a wad of indigestible parts of insects, mostly legs. We found and examined this pellet a few minutes later, while it was still wet. Had I been an expert entomologist, I might have listed almost exactly what the shrike had been eating.

Courtesy the Carnegie Museum of Natural History.

RED-EYED VIREO *(Vireo olivaceus)*

Among the very few Oklahoma birds that sing habitually throughout the day all summer long is the Red-eyed Vireo. There is something restful, even soporific, about the singing during the noon hour. The shady woods have a kind of coolness at that time no matter what the air temperature actually is. Listening to the slightly monotonous pronouncements, we have a feeling that they are given not in defense of nest territory, not, indeed, in defense of anything, but rather as a declaration of comfort or of acceptability of habitat. Translated freely, the phrases might read: *The trees are tall here. Here there is shade. Here peace and quiet. Here caterpillars.* No phrase is long or involved, no phrase quite like the one just preceding it.

Tallness of trees is important. The Red-eyed Vireo does not, according to my observations, nest in the uniform blackjack-post oak woods that are so characteristic of central Oklahoma. It obviously prefers the taller ash, elm, hickory, and pecan trees growing close to streams. You may hear a Red-eye singing while you're among the oaks, but find the bird and it will likely be in another kind of tree.

If you follow the singer about, you will observe that its behavior matches its singing. It moves deliberately from twig to twig. A caterpillar is spied, seized, whacked against a twig until motionless, and gulped; or, if young vireos are to be fed, off goes the dangling morsel to the nest, a beautifully made, thin-walled cup suspended from a forking of twigs toward the end of a horizontal branch ten or so feet from the ground. If you find the nest, the old birds close in on you. Thoroughly disturbed, they snarl with a nasal *nee-ang* as their red eyes flash. They may even dart at you with crown feathers lifted and bills snapping.

The three or four eggs are white, sparsely spotted with dark brown. The nest is often cowbird-parasitized. On the ground under many a nest I have found vireo eggs, each with a big, jagged hole in its side. It is the female cowbird's custom to throw an owner's egg out before laying one of her own.

Young Red-eyes are brown-eyed when they leave the nest, so if you see a Red-eye with brown eyes in late summer you may safely assume that the bird is young. Both young and old males sing occasionally in the fall, songs of young birds being somewhat squeaky.

The Red-eye rarely nests in town. The town vireo is the slightly smaller, less boldly marked Warbling Vireo *(V. gilvus)*, whose eyes are dark brown and whose long, sputtery song is sung high in shade trees along quiet streets and in parks as well as in open woods away from town.

Courtesy the Carnegie Museum of Natural History.

NASHVILLE WARBLER *(Vermivora ruficapilla)*

Inclusion of the Nashville Warbler in a work of this sort is based on data accumulated during half a century of fieldwork. The species migrates through Oklahoma in great numbers in both spring and fall, there being records for virtually every county in which much fieldwork has been done. In other words, the Nashville Warbler is among Oklahoma's commonest birds, even though it does not nest here.

The species is distinguishable at all seasons by the yellow of its chin, throat, and breast, the gray and olive of its upperparts, *and its white eye-ring*. Females are less colorful than males, and young males in their first winter plumage are less clearly marked than adult males. Spring males are gray on the upper part of the head; the crown has a reddish brown crown-patch; and the white of the eye-ring is conspicuous. In young males in the fall the gray of the head is veiled with brown, the yellow of the underparts is somewhat buffy, and the brown of the crown-patch is vague and more or less concealed. Young birds, especially young females, are sometimes difficult to identify with certainty, though the yellow of the underparts is always clear and the eyering is always there. To be borne in mind is the fact that the wings are without bars and the tail has no white at its corners.

Warblers likely to be confused with the Nashville in Oklahoma are the Tennessee *(V. peregrina)*, which has a white line over the eye but no eye-ring, and which is plain white below in the spring and never more than faintly yellowish below in the fall; and the Orange-crowned *(V. celata)*, a dull-colored species whose underparts are yellowish gray, whose eye is not ringed with white, and whose orange crown is rarely visible in the field if it is there at all. Neither the Tennessee nor the Orange-crown is really common in Oklahoma as a rule, though both occur in spring and fall and the Orange-crown occasionally shows up in winter. The Orange-crown is sometimes yellow enough below to look like a Nashville, but it does not have even a faint white eye-ring.

The songs of the three species are similar, that of the Nashville sounding to me like *witzy, witzy, witzy, chi-chi-chi-chi*, in other words a two-syllabled phrase repeated three times followed by a sort of buzz. The Tennessee's song is more complex, having three sorts of sounds instead of two: *witzy, witzy, tsipa, tsipa, chi-chi-chi-chi*. The Orangecrown's song is a slightly warbled series of *tsips*, rather like the rushedthrough song of a Chipping Sparrow *(Spizella passerina)*.

Courtesy the Carnegie Museum of Natural History.

YELLOW WARBLER *(Dendroica petechia)*

The mid-summer distribution of this warbler in Oklahoma is puzzling. In the northeastern United States, where I spent much of my earlier life, the Yellow Warbler was common not only in orchards and along the edges of woodlands but also in towns. In Oklahoma I hardly know where to look for it in summer, though I know it's here.

I see Yellow Warblers during every period of migration, especially in fall, but finding breeding pairs has never been easy. Nowhere have I found them nesting in someone's yard or garden. The only nests I have found in the Norman area have been at Hospital Lake, a comparatively "wild" area along the city's northeast edge. The several nestings there, never more than one or two per summer, have been in trees well above ground. In the meadowlike area below Fort Supply Reservoir in Woodward County, a small population has bred regularly. In the spring of 1976, in Methodist Canyon near the city of Hinton, members of the Oklahoma Ornithological Society watched a female bird building a nest well up in a large cottonwood not far from a small stream.

The only good-sized breeding populations that I have found have been along the Cimarron River at the west end of the Panhandle. There the species has bred regularly during the past forty years. Nests that I found were in sapling cottonwoods; but I suspect that many were in willows and salt cedar.

Nests are neat, well-built cups firmly attached to upright twigs as a rule. The eggs, usually three or four, are white with gray flecking, principally at the larger end. Young birds at the time they leave the nest are ashy gray except for the yellowish-olive edging of the incoming large wing and tail feathers. The postjuvenal molt is rapid. By the time the bird's first tail feathers are full length, the gray plumage of the head and body has been largely replaced by the first winter plumage. The bird is now yellow, generally speaking, especially on the underparts, and it has one diagnostic feature worth bearing in mind: all but the middle tail feathers are yellow on their inner webs, thus giving the tail a truly yellow appearance when spread. In this respect *Dendroica petechia* is unique among wood warblers. No other species of the family flashes real yellow from its spread tail as it flies off.

Throughout much of its breeding range, the Yellow Warbler is heavily parasitized by the cowbird. In trying to rid itself of the pest, the female warblers have been known to build many-layered nests, each buried layer of which contains at least one cowbird egg. I have not, since coming to Oklahoma in 1952, observed a parasitized nest, nor have I seen an adult Yellow Warbler caring for a young cowbird.

YELLOW-RUMPED WARBLER *(Dendroica coronata)*

One winter day I happened upon a Yellow-rumped Warbler in a juniper tree that was loaded with ripe blue berries. The warbler was doing its best to find a berry small enough to swallow. The growing season must have been good, for all the berries were big. The bird picked off berry after berry, working hard to get one past the corners of its mouth, but not one berry was small enough. After about twenty tries (twenty berries, that is), the warbler gave up. I started to say *with disgust*, but disgust is what *I* felt. All of those thousands upon thousands of berries, and not one small enough to swallow!

I knew what species the warbler was, for I could see the big yellow patch on its rump and the small yellow patch on each side of its chest. The yellow crown-patch that I knew it had I did not see, for it never showed me the top of its head. The throat was plain white, so I knew that the bird belonged to the eastern subspecies, the form that used to be called the Myrtle Warbler. Had its throat been yellow, I'd have known that it belonged to the western race, the form that used to be called the Audubon's Warbler. Both of these races migrate through and winter in Oklahoma, the white-throated one all over the state, the yellow-throated one chiefly in the western half. Each race is much less colorful in winter than in summer.

A few Yellow-rumped Warblers are among the earliest of southward-moving migrants in the fall; but most of them come later. They go about in scattered companies as a rule, often with the roving flocks of small birds that forage in the winter woods.

In severe winter weather, especially during ice-storms, insect-eating birds have a hard time finding food. During bad spells in Norman, Yellow-rumped Warblers have repeatedly been found dead, almost certainly from starvation and exposure. Specimens that I have examined have, as a rule, been very thin, and very little food was in their stomachs. At a bird-feeder in Georgia, in the early spring of 1952, I saw many insect-eating birds feeding eagerly on pecan meats. The nuts had been hastily cracked, but the birds had no trouble extricating the edible bits. Cracked pecans put out in bad weather, and kept free of ice, can sometimes tide the birds over.

Toward the end of winter Yellow-rumped Warblers undergo an extensive molt into their breeding plumage. For a time they have a bedraggled appearance; but presently they become very colorful. Now the yellow patch at each side of the chest is conspicuous, for it is set-off by black. About this time the male birds begin to sing, too. The song is gentle, unmusical, and not at all noticeable. Spring migration takes the birds northward almost to tree-limit in Alaska and Canada and to high elevations in the Rocky Mountain cordillera.

Courtesy the Carnegie Museum of Natural History.

COMMON YELLOWTHROAT *(Geothlypis trichas)*

This wood warbler breeds more widely in Oklahoma than any other member of its family except possibly the Yellow Warbler *(Dendroica petechia)* and Yellow-breasted Chat *(Icteria virens)*. The reason for this is that marshy places, its preferred habitat, are scattered here and there in all sorts of terrain—at ponds in parks and open cattle range, along the edges of slow-moving woodland streams, in low-lying spots below dams—in short, wherever cattails, bulrushes, sedge, or other tall aquatic vegetation flourishes. For plants to provide this habitat, a more or less constant water-level is requisite. Occasionally the species nests away from water in old fields or among tall ragweed and bone-set in shady places along the woodland edge. Often such a pair nests quite by itself; as a rule, however, where the right habitat is available several pairs nest not far from each other.

Wherever the bird is nesting, its song, a rhythmic repetition of some such phrase as *wichitty* or *witchery*, is a familiar sound. Singing does not continue all day on hot days in midsummer, but scattered songs are to be heard well into July and August, for two broods per season are reared regularly in Oklahoma.

The adult male Common Yellowthroat wears at all seasons a bold black facial mask. Just back of the mask is a strip of gray. The back, wings, and tail are olive. The yellow of the throat extends over the breast, upper belly, and under tail coverts; the lower belly is white. Young males wear a mask, once the fluffy nestling plumage has been replaced, but it is veiled with gray. Females are without bold markings of any sort, and they vary greatly in color, some being buffy rather than yellow on the throat and breast, some quite brown on the top of the head. A call note given by both sexes is a fairly distinct *chack*.

The species "squeaks up" readily, so if you keep yourself hidden you may get a good look at the bird. And if you are lucky, you may witness a flight-song. Now the male flies upward several feet and sings his *witchery, witchery, witchery, witch* very plainly from start to finish, then drops back down to the cattails. It is a pretty performance.

The nest, of grass, is well hidden in vegetation not far above the water or wet ground. It is lined with fine grasses (no hair, no feathers). If already built, it is hard to find, for the female slips off quietly and does not display anxiety through scolding. The three to five eggs are creamy white, marked with dark spots and scrawls chiefly at the larger end.

Courtesy the Carnegie Museum of Natural History.

WILSON'S WARBLER *(Wilsonia pusilla)*

Bird students who live in the eastern United States are used to seeing treefuls of wood warblers when migration is on in full force. Any tree may have several kinds of warblers in it, some easy to identify, some not so easy. Your confirmed warbler enthusiast remembers which species are difficult, so knows just what to look for. I recall many an autumn day in West Virginia when I was sorely confused by the similarity of the scores of Bay-breasted Warblers *(Dendroica castanea)* to the scores of Blackpoll Warblers *(D. striata)* passing through at the same time. Immature birds of the two species looked very much alike. I finally decided that an important distinguishing feature was the Blackpoll's yellowish tarsi and toes. If a bird with yellowish looking legs had no buffy brown tinge on its flanks, then that bird was a Blackpoll. If it had dark legs and some buffy brown on the flanks it was a Bay-breast.

Oklahoma's warblers aren't much of a problem as a rule, because there aren't many warblers. When I first moved to Norman I couldn't understand why my daily birdlists in the fall included so few warblers. *Where are they, or what's wrong with me?* I asked myself.

The fact is that, although several warbler species nest in eastern Oklahoma, many of these do not migrate through the state in great numbers either in spring or fall. They seem to disappear about the time the breeding season ends. If they are seen at all they are seen in the eastern third of the state. The transient warblers that are seen in great numbers in Oklahoma nest not in Oklahoma but either well north of Oklahoma or at considerable elevation in the Rocky Mountains.

Among warblers that migrate through Oklahoma in great numbers is the Wilson's Warbler, a species sometimes called the Black-capped Warbler. It is equally abundant in all wooded parts of the state in both spring and fall. It is easy to identify as a rule because it is confiding, it "squeaks up" readily, and its color pattern is simple. Adult birds do not molt into a special winter plumage. The species is yellow throughout the face and underparts and olive above; it has neither eye-ring nor wingbars; and it has a longish unmarked tail that "wags" a bit, gnat-catcherwise, as if loosely attached to the body. Adult males have a noticeable black cap. In adult females the cap is sometimes inconspicuous. In young birds in first winter plumage there is no cap at all. They are plain olive above and plain yellow below and are sometimes a bit difficult to identify.

Courtesy the Carnegie Museum of Natural History.

THE MEADOWLARKS

There are two kinds of meadowlarks in Oklahoma, the Eastern *(Sturnella magna)* and the Western *(S. neglecta)*. The two are very much alike in size, shape, and color, but strikingly different in song and certain other vocalizations. The color differences, which show up best in adult males, are these: in the Eastern the bright yellow of the under side of the head is strictly confined to the chin and throat, whereas in the Western it spreads onto the malar region, thus making the head a little more colorful. The malar region in the Eastern is white, a feature that can be seen in the field through a good binocular. In female birds and young males this encroachment of the yellow onto the malar region is sometimes hard to see, even with specimens in hand, so the character is not always useful. The other difference is apparent in the tail feathers and inner secondary wing feathers. In the Eastern these large feathers are brownish black in the middle from base to tip; in the Western the dark middle part is crossed by light brown bars. This barring can be seen in the field under ideal light conditions; but it must be remembered that in some Eastern Meadowlarks the dark middle part is less wide than in others, and in some Western Meadowlarks the light cross-barring is obscure. In all Eastern Meadowlarks these important wing and tail feathers are barred to some extent, but the barring does not cross the dark middle part.

Song and call note differences may be summed up thus: the song of the Eastern is a high, simple, whistled *dee-oo, dee-ay*, the last syllable longer than the others. The Western "sings up a storm" by comparison; its performance has many syllables, some of them fairly gurgled. The sentence "I'll steal your wheat, young man" is an evocative attempt to transliterate the song of the Western. One alarm call of the Western is a loud, rapid *tur, tur, tur, tur!* Alarmed Easterns chatter.

Both species inhabit open pastureland. The Eastern breeds throughout the main body of Oklahoma, in forested areas being confined to clearings, in western counties to low-lying grassy meadows along the larger rivers. I have not thus far found a breeding population of Easterns in the Panhandle; but in the somewhat marshy area below Fort Supply Reservoir several Easterns regularly nest, surrounded by comparatively high, dry cattle range in which the Western thrives.

In winter great numbers of Western Meadowlarks move into the state. Since both Easterns and Westerns sing at any time of year, it is often possible to compare the songs directly.

Meadowlark nests are on the ground in or under grass and are somewhat domed over. The four or five eggs are white, speckled with reddish brown chiefly at the larger end. Only the female incubates, but both the male and female feed the young. Young birds often leave the nest before they can fly. Their food-call is a high, thin squeal that carries well, though it is not very loud.

RED-WINGED BLACKBIRD *(Agelaius phoeniceus)*

A huge blackbird roost near Norman in the winter of 1952–53 was the talk of the countryside. The thousands of birds that gathered night after night were mostly Redwings, but a few were Brown-headed Cowbirds and Starlings. Most of the Redwings by far were males. The Redwings and cowbirds roosted in coarse, head-high, dead switchgrass in low parts of the Canadian River's floodplain, the Starlings in trees close by. When I first visited the roost on January 10, a disagreeable stench pervaded the area and a thin layer of droppings covered the ground.

Interested persons visited the roost with me several times between January 10 and February 4, sometimes in late afternoon, to watch the birds fly in, sometimes in the early morning twilight, sometimes at night, armed with scoop-nets, flashlights, and banding equipment. The first flocks to arrive alighted not in the grass, but in trees. As more flocks came, the trees became black. Overloaded trees would suddenly "explode," and the masses would distribute themselves in other trees. Not until darkness threatened did the birds descend to the grass. Hordes that continued to arrive during half-light were encouraged by murmuring from the grass, so trailed downward without alighting in trees.

We learned that the birds did not sleep on the ground but while clinging to stout grass stalks a few inches up. Scattered bunches of feathers were evidence not of molt but of predation. On every visit we found dead and crippled birds and often saw an opossum, raccoon, or feral house cat.

Especially memorable was one windless night when we planned to band as many birds as possible. The air was colder at the roost than on higher ground back from the floodplain. We stomped around doing our best to keep warm while the birds quieted down. When finally we rushed the roost with nets we caught far more birds than we had bands for. Running through the grass was difficult, but the flying birds were bewildered, so we caught them not only in the nets but with our hands, snatching them as they collided with each other. In the distance we heard squeals from birds caught by predatory mammals or owls. Several of us saw a gray fox as it bounded off. Air fanned down by the rising multitude was surprisingly warm.

The Redwing nests in marshy places as a rule, often above water in cattails, bulrushes, or willows. The three or four light blue eggs are marked with black spots, blotches and scrawls. The female builds the nest and incubates the eggs. The species summers locally throughout Oklahoma. Where there is no marsh they may nest in a lush meadow, alfalfa field, or stand of salt cedar. Two broods are reared.

Courtesy Field Enterprises Educational Corporation.

NORTHERN ORIOLE *(Icterus galbula)*

The tag-end of summer is too often considered a poor time for bird study. True, the robins that hunt for worms on the lawn are ragged from molting, the Painted Buntings have stopped singing, and some birds in changing plumage are unlike anything pictured in the bird books. But the trained ear listens for the bubbled *whee-di-lee* of a migrating Upland Sandpiper *(Bartramia longicauda)* high in the sky; the eager bird student goes to the mudflats where shorebirds galore are feeding; and the quick of eye sees the flash of orange, black, and white of an adult male Northern Oriole as it flies from one tree to another. Not all is lost: dullness of season is in the heart and mind of him who stays indoors.

The gorgeous male oriole has completed his annual molt. His full-length tail, fanned wide, is black in the middle, orange at the corners. Squeak him down from the treetop and he scolds. His voice is harsh, almost rasping. Having given you a long, hard look, he returns to the treetop where he sings two or three rich, violin-clear notes. Nesting was over weeks ago. As the young birds learned to fend for themselves the parent birds drifted apart.

At winter's end the orioles return—first the bright males, then the females, some of which are puzzling, for the amount of black on the head varies from bird to bird. Fervent singing from the males declares suitability of habitat, pairs form, and presently the females are busy building nests. These usually are hung near the ends of long drooping branches.

The four to six eggs are white, thinly spotted and scrawled with black. The young are silent during the first week of their lives, but toward the end of the fledging period they become quite vocal. It is possible to locate all of an area's Northern Oriole nests by listening for the musical calling of the almost-fledged young.

By sheer coincidence an adult male Northern Oriole has just flown into a juniper a few yards from the window near which I write. The date is July 31. The bird is after bagworms. I love watching him partly because he is so beautiful, partly because he knows how to deal with this cordially hated pest. He knows that he cannot tear apart the tough bag. He knows that if he alights clumsily near a bag the larva inside will feel the shaking of the twig and make itself unobtainable. So he quietly climbs from twig to twig waiting to see the moving head of a larva sticking out of one of the bags. Now does he lunge, grasp, and keep on grasping, quite literally crushing the larva to death. He may not be able to pull his prey out, but he can sip its juice. If only, I say to myself, that oriole would stay long enough to dispatch every larva!

COMMON GRACKLE *(Quiscalus quiscula)*

More than faintly ironic has been the bird problem I've had at my house, on West Brooks Street in Norman. On my side of the street is a row of three large hackberry trees in which blackbirds have roosted by the thousand summer after summer. The blackbirds have been Brown-headed Cowbirds, Starlings, Common Grackles, and Great-tailed Grackles, in that order of abundance. So numerous have they been that their droppings have covered the sidewalks, smeared parked cars, and obliged people walking under the trees to hold newspapers over their heads. While the birds foregather, jostle for perches, and sleep, they also molt, so feathers have come down with the droppings. The irony of it all is that I'm known to be a student, lover, and protector of birds. "Why don't you do something that will make those birds roost somewhere else?" is a question that has never been asked aloud, though I've read it on many a face.

I have observed that frightening the birds from my part of town merely gives the problem to someone else. I've learned to lessen the numbers that roost near me by dropping a big fiber tray on the sidewalk in such a way as to produce a loud, sharp, resounding clatter. If I start dropping the tray early in the evening, the epicenter of the roost shifts, sometimes considerably. But it's not easy to be at home every evening at the critical time, and the tray has all too often been ineffectual. Chagrined over my inability to "tray" the birds off, I have telephoned the police.

Shooting sessions have been noisy, more or less effective, and to some extent lethal. We haven't tried to kill the birds, but some have died. Specimens that I have preserved for the university's collection have shown interesting stages of the molt. All adult Common Grackle specimens killed on a given date have shown that the replacement of feathers was proceeding in about the same way throughout the whole population.

Summer after summer I have wondered where the Common Grackles of the roost have come from. There have been many small nesting colonies in the city. A few pairs nested one summer near the top of the big cedar of Lebanon near my house; that same year another small colony nested high in an elm about a block away. I have located the colonies by watching the female birds carrying nest material. At colonies that I have observed closely the birds have reared only one brood in a season.

The Common Grackle breeds statewide. Near the New Mexico line a colony has nested year after year in the framework of an iron bridge over a major tributary to the Cimarron just west of Kenton. A separate nest that I found recently in that area was in a cavity in a fairly large dead tree.

Courtesy the Carnegie Museum of Natural History.

BROWN-HEADED COWBIRD *(Molothrus ater)*

It is easy to hate the cowbird, whose custom it is to lay its eggs in other birds' nests. The hatred seems justifiable enough as we watch a pair of Cardinals slaving away for a brood composed wholly of cowbirds; when we find an Orchard Oriole's nest bulging with two or three cowbirds and one oriole; or when, during several seasons of careful observation, we witness the gradual disappearance of a Bell's Vireo population from an extensive plum thicket that has been visited by too many female cowbirds spring after spring.

The above is no over-statement. So similar are cowbird eggs to those of the Cardinal that even if the female Cardinal wants to rid her nest of cowbird eggs she may throw her own out by mistake. So tightly woven is the Orchard Oriole's nest that whatever hatches there remains until it fledges if it can reach high enough to claim a fair share of food, the trouble being that often there is only one oriole egg left to hatch after the cowbirds have replaced oriole eggs with their own. As for the Bell's Vireo, that species is made to order for the cowbird's use: its nests are low and easy to find and the vireos so often rear one or more cowbirds *but no vireo* that the vireo fails to reproduce itself. The cowbird wins, but it also loses. Were there not other "hosts" to turn to, it would be done-for as a species.

According to my observations during the past twenty-odd years, the Cardinal is the cowbird's perfect "host" in Oklahoma, for the Cardinal usually rears at least one of its own young along with one, two, or three cowbirds. Parasitism does not, in other words, eliminate the Cardinal.

Not an altogether pleasant state of affairs, it would seem. But consider the wonder of it: females of a whole wide-ranging species shorn of any urge to build their own nests, incubate eggs, or care for young; males with no territory to find, stake out, and defend with song, no young to feed! In a very real sense of the phrase, reproduction without parenthood.

Yet every spring I listen eagerly for the squeaky song that announces the cowbird's return. I look up to see a single male, two males, or perhaps a close-knit flock of three to five males and one female flying not far overhead. The flock alights on a bare branch. The urge to perform leads one male to bow extravagantly with widespread wings and tail. So ridiculous is the "act" that it seems accidental; but no, there it goes again, another bow just as overdone as the first, but by another male. The female, if female there be, seems unimpressed. Presently she flies off, followed by all of the males. If there are males only, they bow to each other.

CARDINAL *(Cardinalis cardinalis)*

The brightness of a male Cardinal is especially welcome on a cold winter day. Fluffed up to retain body heat, he flies to the feeding counter. Here he concentrates on sunflower seeds, picking each up with his powerful mandibles, working it around until it is "on edge," and splitting it open. It is winter, remember. The pair-bond is not very strong. His mate, a dull-colored bird, is off in the shrubbery waiting for him to finish. The minute he flies off, she flies in.

The Cardinal's song is a whistled repetition of such English words as *what cheer* or *wet year* or, occasionally, the Spanish word *cierto* (pronounced see-air-toe). Several Cardinals in my neighborhood have been singing *cierto* recently. I suspect that they have learned the sound from each other. Both male and female sing, the male the year round, the female not, as a rule, until there is promise of spring and the male begins to court. Now, instead of keeping her away from the feeding counter, he feeds her, making something of a ceremony of it all, with sunflower seeds cracked by none other than himself.

Courtship feeding I have observed repeatedly in February and March. Some nests are started in late March, but eggs are not usually laid until the first week of April. Nests are rather fragile structures of dead weed stems, leaf skeletons, and bits of paper, lined with rootlets and strips of grapevine bark. The female builds the nest by herself, finding and carrying in material unaccompanied by her mate. Nor is she fed by him during the thirteen-day incubation period. It is quite possible that he does not even know where the nest is while it is being built and while it holds eggs.

When the young hatch, the male becomes aware of them gradually, at first bringing food that the female has to break up into bits small enough for the little mouths; but he learns in time to feed the young himself, and eventually he takes full charge of the first brood while the female goes ahead with a second. As a rule she builds a new nest for the second brood.

Recently fledged young Cardinals of both sexes resemble their mother, differing from her chiefly in having dark, more or less colorless, rather than orange-pink bills. They follow their father about while his mate proceeds with the second nesting. Shortly after the young males have learned to fend for themselves they begin to turn red. With their molt into first winter feather they become almost as bright as their father.

The Cardinal is strictly non-migratory. It is common in Oklahoma westward to the Panhandle. A few pairs breed as far west as Guymon; but west of that city it has been recorded only once, so far as I know—a female bird seen along the Cimarron River 13 miles north of Boise City on November 27, 1960.

PAINTED BUNTING *(Passerina ciris)*

Many a Painted Bunting kills itself flying into a window. If the bird is an adult male, its bright colors bewilder the person who finds it. When brought to me, its bearer says: "Of course this bird couldn't have come from around here. It's tropical. Where do you suppose it came from, and how did it get here?" I am obliged to say that the Painted Bunting is fairly common in Oklahoma, but that it isn't often seen.

Norman has grown a lot within the past twenty years. I have to go to the country now to see a Painted Bunting. And even when I get to a place where I know the bird lives, I have to wait a while before I hear its cheerful song. The woods are mixed; there's a farm pond not far off, but the rolling land is well drained; there are no willows, no stands of tall weeds. I know the bird is on a wire along a road or at the top of a small tree. I have in mind the bright red underparts, purplish blue head, and bright green back; then I remember that first-year males also sing and that they are olive above and dull grayish yellow below, much like the female. I become a bit impatient, since I can't see the singer. Then I see him, or part of him; up goes the binocular; I glimpse a flash of red, and off goes the bird. It *was* an adult male, I mumble, and find myself sympathizing with the many persons who have told me that they have "looked and looked" but have never really seen a Painted Bunting.

The female builds the nest unaided by the male, though she may be encouraged by his singing. The nest is a neat, thin-walled cup of plant fibers, slender dry weed-stems, and leaf skeletons bound together by cobweb. Often it is on a downward slanted branch in the lower part of a tree or in a vine in a shaded place. The eggs, usually four, are white with brown flecks chiefly at the larger end. Often the nest holds one or more cowbird eggs and about the same number of bunting eggs. When the first brood for the season leaves the nest, the male takes charge of them while the female proceeds with a second nesting.

The adult male Painted Bunting continues to be bright throughout the year; he has no dull winter plumage. Adult males are rarely seen in Oklahoma after the first week of August. Perhaps they go into retirement and molt before migrating, but I suspect that they migrate first, then molt. The species winters from Mexico southward to Panama and also in the West Indies.

DICKCISSEL *(Spiza americana)*

The word *dickcissel* imitates this prairie bird's song, though for me the average song has four syllables rather than three: *dick, chick-chick-chick*. The performance varies geographically. In driving across northern Oklahoma in the summer of 1937 I passed through one area in which the song was *dick, plick, chick-chick-chick*, a lengthening that I couldn't help noticing, for every bird, mile after mile, had adopted it.

Along roads through pastureland or between alfalfa fields most of the singing is from telephone wires. Where there are no wires the top of a weed or bush serves as a song perch. Only the males sing, and singing continues until the last of July, then stops abruptly, whether young of delayed or second broods have left the nest or not. A call note often heard in late summer is a clearly enunciated *djjjj*.

Dickcissels may be hard to find in fall even close to areas in which they have nested. A favorite habitat at that season is a dense stand of tall grass or weeds—the sort of place a person usually walks around rather than through. Here literally dozens of the birds may gather, young and old. While molting, they form close-knit flocks, preparing for migration southward. In the species' winter home—from southern Mexico southward to northern South America—big flocks go romping about high in air then suddenly drop en masse to a favorite feeding, drinking, or bathing spot. In Colima, southwestern Mexico, I watched flocks of this sort day after day in mid-January of 1971 before seeing the birds clearly enough to realize what they were.

When Dickcissels return to their breeding grounds in spring, the males announce arrival with song. Migration is at its height in early May. One night at the Tulsa airport in early May of 1947, when my flight southward was cancelled because of severe wind, I saw hundreds of Dickcissels that probably had been lured down from the sky by the bright lights. Doing their best to stay on the landing strip despite the wind, the buffeted birds reminded me of autumn leaves. At first I thought they were all House Sparrows; then I saw the black and yellow on the throats and knew they were Dickcissels.

Dickcissel nests are rather bulky structures made of dead weedstems and grass and lined with fine grass. They are on the ground or in alfalfa, between tough weedstalks, or in shrubbery or small trees from two to 14 feet up. The three to six unmarked eggs are pale blue. A remarkable "double" nest that I found in south-central Oklahoma on June 18, 1959, had one Dickcissel egg and one cowbird egg in the upper nest and four Dickcissel eggs in the lower. Between the two nests, which were about a foot apart, was a shaggy mass of material that served as foundation for the upper and as roof for the lower. The eggs that were being incubated were in the lower nest, which presumably had been built after desertion of the upper.

AMERICAN GOLDFINCH *(Carduelis tristis)*

In winter people often ask me about a "really little bird with black-and-white wings and tail, brown upperparts, and some yellow on the face" that's been visiting their bird-feeder. I counter with a question about what they mean by "really little." When they say that the bird is "quite a bit smaller than an English Sparrow" I know they have been seeing an American Goldfinch *in winter plumage.*

The species is especially interesting because it is so much commoner here in winter than in summer and because it has about a thousand more feathers in winter than in summer. The change from winter to summer plumage is striking, but it takes place gradually, never giving the bird a bedraggled appearance. Goldfinches nest not in spring but in summer, so that while many other birds are rearing broods the goldfinches are busy molting. The change in color is much more noticeable in males than in females. The males lose the brown and gray winter plumage, becoming a luminous yellow both above and below save for the black of the cap and the white of the lower back, rump, belly, and under tail coverts. The wings and tail stay black-and-white all year.

No part of Oklahoma is without goldfinches in winter; but in summer the species' distribution is puzzlingly spotty. Indeed, I know of only a few localities where the species has been known to breed summer after summer. Near Norman, a very few pairs have bred at Hospital Lake. Pairs have summered fairly regularly at Red Rock Canyon State Park near Hinton, in the low-lying area below Fort Supply Reservoir in Woodward County, in open woods in the northeastern corner of the state, and along the Cimarron River near Boise City and Kenton at the west end of the Panhandle. But very few nests have been found, and I suspect that many birds seen in summer do not have nests, despite their being in breeding plumage.

The American Goldfinch's flight is strongly undulatory. With each bound the bird calls *per-sits-so-ree.* As it changes from winter to summer plumage it begins to sing. Its songs, which are bright, tuneful, and sometimes long, are so complex that they cannot be imitated at all accurately with human syllables. Flight-singing is part of courtship. While the female is building the nest, laying the eggs, and incubating them, the male often circles the nest, singing rapturously.

The nest is so thick-walled and compact that it holds water—sometimes a serious handicap, for if it fills, the small chicks drown. Nests are sometimes low, in shrubbery, sometimes high in a tall tree at the forest's edge. The eggs, which number four to six, are very pale blue and unspotted. Egg-laying usually starts late, sometimes as late as mid-July, after the cowbird's egg-laying season has passed. Young goldfinches are fed by regurgitation.

Courtesy the Carnegie Museum of Natural History.

FIELD SPARROW *(Spizella pusilla)*

V. J. Vacin, of Oklahoma City, was an enthusiastic bird-bander for many years. Among the most interesting birds handled at his Silver Lake banding station was a Field Sparrow banded there on March 29, 1958, and recaptured at the very same place on December 29, 1958, February 13, 1960, February 11, 1961, December 29, 1961, December 20, 1963, and January 30, 1965. Since the Field Sparrow is not known to nest as early as March anywhere within its range, the bird must have been at least a year old when banded. It was therefore at least seven years old when last handled—not bad for a little creature weighing about 14 grams that could have traveled a long, long way between visits to Silver Lake.

I must not overdramatize. The Field Sparrow is not one of those world travelers that move "from zone to zone" in their migrations. The bird that my friend handled might have nested within only a few hundred yards of the spot at which it was banded. This possibility does not derogate from what I have said above, for even in Oklahoma seven years of battling with weather, predators, etc., can be touch and go.

The Field Sparrow inhabits unforested parts of Oklahoma westward to the 100th meridian virtually all year. In the shinnery country of Ellis and Roger Mills counties it is fairly common. Nowhere does it nest in the Panhandle, however, except possibly at the easternmost end. Nowhere have I seen it at any season west of Rosston, in Harper County, and Gate, in Beaver County.

The species is not boldly marked. The pink of its bill is a good field mark, but its light eye-ring and two white wing-bars are not very noticeable. One behavior trait is important: the bird "squeaks up" readily at all seasons, even when molting. I have noted repeatedly that when I conceal myself and "squeak" loudly, Field Sparrows are often the very first birds to respond. When they do fly in, they usually sit still for a bit, allowing close inspection with the binocular.

The Field Sparrow's song is exquisite. It is a series of short whistles, all often at the same high pitch, that becomes a sort of trill at the end. It has considerable carrying power. Many a person who follows the song about is surprised at the smallness of the singer.

The nest, a neat little cup of fine dead weed stalks, lined with fine grass, is placed on the ground or in a shrub or small tree from a few inches to several feet up. The two to five eggs are pale greenish blue, heavily speckled with light brown, chiefly at the larger end. The species is often cowbird-parasitized. Two broods are reared as a rule. Second nests for the season are usually built well above ground.

George Miksch Sutton

Courtesy the Carnegie Museum of Natural History.

HARRIS'S SPARROW *(Zonotrichia querula)*

In the summer of 1931, almost a century after this large, handsome sparrow had been formally described, I discovered its eggs. The nest was on the ground in spruce woods near the mouth of the Churchill River, on the west coast of Hudson Bay. I had seen the bird there the preceding fall, so felt sure that if I could get there in early summer and work hard enough, I'd find the nest. Ours was a four-man expedition from the Carnegie Museum in Pittsburgh. We all worked hard. I shall never forget the strange effect the big black letters HARRIS on a box upside down along the railroad right-of-way had on me shortly before the discovery. How could those letters be anything but a good omen? Harris was the name of a meat-packing firm in Canada.

As a youngster living near the Texas Christian University campus at Fort Worth, I saw much of the Harris's Sparrow in winter. In woods not far from our house it was common. I loved its conversational *peebly, peebly* calls, its sharp *weenk* of alarm, and its fragile whistling. I perceived that there was much variation in the amount of black on the crown, face, throat, and chest. Some birds were white-throated, others white on the lower throat but black on the chin. Some birds with white throat had much black on the chest and sides. Blackest of all on the crown, face, and throat were freshly-molted birds ready to leave for the north in spring. And every one of them, no matter how much black it had, also had a pink bill.

According to my recent observations in Oklahoma, both male and female birds give the *peebly, peebly* call, often in a sort of chorus; but I suspect that the delicate whistling that issues from a tangle of wild grape or greenbriar on a bright, windless day, and that is heard so often on the breeding grounds, is done by the males.

If two or three Harris's Sparrows fly up ahead of you, remember that they usually alight well above ground, where they may perch quietly not far from each other for some time if undisturbed. If you will train your binocular on them, seeing what you can through the brush without moving around much trying to get a clearer look, you will see first of all the pink bill, then the black on the crown, the black streaks on the chest and sides, and the two white wingbars. Perhaps you will see the bill of one bird, the crown of another, the underparts of a third.

Zonotrichia querula winters throughout Oklahoma. Though commonest in the central and northeastern parts of the state, it has been seen westward in small numbers as far as the New Mexico state line. For some reason it seems to be uncommon in the southeastern corner of the state. Just before it departs for the north in spring, it molts heavily about the head.

LINCOLN'S SPARROW *(Melospiza lincolnii)*

Including this elusive, not often clearly seen bird in a work of this sort may surprise some readers; but I have come to think of the Lincoln's Sparrow as one of Oklahoma's truly common birds. Not since I have lived in Norman have I failed to see it in my yard year after year. I have often heard it singing in spring (never in fall or winter). The song is not loud, nor do its phrases call to mind human words or syllables. It bubbles away at about three levels, first a low one, then a higher, then a higher still, ending with a terse summary of all three. Often it reminds me a bit of a House Wren's song.

The male does not, according to my experience on the bird's nesting ground, as well as in various parts of Oklahoma, regularly sing from the top of a tall weed or bush, but keeps fairly well hidden. Indeed, what one usually sees of the Lincoln's Sparrow is one clear look just after it has been "squeaked up," then brief glimpses as it flits out from low in a hedge and darts in again. *Elusive* is the word.

If the bird is clearly visible the *grayness* of its face is apparent. There is brown on the crown, ear coverts, back, wings, and tail, to be sure, and buff on the malar stripe, but the grayness of the area above the eye is noticeable. Then, if the underparts are at all visible, the strongly buffy band across the chest, plus the dark streaking there and on the sides and flanks, make clear at once what the species is. The buffy chest-band is stressed in all the books, and this diagnostic feature is a good one, but the grayness of the face is perceptible much more often than the buffy chest-band is: that is my reason for stressing it here.

Look for the bird in hedges, flowerbeds, and shrubbery in towns, and in thickets along dirt roads in the country. If you move quietly along the road, making no effort at all to crash through the brush, you will often see Lincoln's Sparrows flying up ahead of you. It is their custom to alight well above ground, then to fly to a still higher perch, where they sometimes stay long enough for you to scrutinize them. In this behavior they are similar to the Harris's Sparrow, several of which will sometimes alight not far from each other and perch quietly while you look at them through the tangle. If the Harris's stay put, the Lincoln's with them will often stay put also, but don't expect to have much of a look at the buffy chest-band. It's the back and the gray on the face that you'll see.

The Lincoln's alarm note, a soft *chuck*, resembles that of the juncos. It is considerably less loud than the *chuck* of a Fox Sparrow *(Passerella iliaca)* and it does not have the heavy alto (almost baritone) quality of the alarm note of the Song Sparrow *(Melospiza melodia)*.

Courtesy the Carnegie Museum of Natural History.

THE BIRDS OF OKLAHOMA

Bracketed species have never been collected or satisfactorily photographed in Oklahoma.

Common Loon. *Gavia immer.*
[Red-throated Loon. *Gavia stellata.*
[Red-necked Grebe. *Podiceps grisegena.*
Horned Grebe. *Podiceps auritus.*
Eared Grebe. *Podiceps nigricollis.*
Western Grebe. *Aechmophorus occidentalis.*
Pied-billed Grebe. *Podilymbus podiceps.*
White Pelican. *Pelecanus erythrorhynchos.*
Brown Pelican. *Pelecanus occidentalis.*
Double-crested Cormorant. *Phalacrocorax auritus.*
Olivaceous Cormorant. *Phalacrocorax olivaceus.*
Anhinga. *Anhinga anhinga.*
Magnificent Frigatebird. *Fregata magnificens.*
Great Frigatebird. *Fregata minor.*
Great Blue Heron. *Ardea herodias.*
Green Heron. *Butorides striatus.*
Little Blue Heron. *Florida caerulea.*
Cattle Egret. *Bubulcus ibis.*
Great Egret. *Casmerodius albus.*
Snowy Egret. *Egretta thula.*
Louisiana Heron. *Hydranassa tricolor.*
Black-crowned Night Heron. *Nycticorax nycticorax.*
Yellow-crowned Night Heron. *Nyctanassa violacea.*
Least Bittern. *Ixobrychus exilis.*
American Bittern. *Botaurus lentiginosus.*
Wood Stork. *Mycteria americana.*
Jabiru. *Jabiru mycteria.*
Glossy Ibis. *Plegadis falcinellus.*
White-faced Ibis. *Plegadis chihi.*
White Ibis. *Eudocimus albus.*
Roseate Spoonbill. *Ajaia ajaja.*
[Mute Swan. *Cygnus olor.*
Whistling Swan. *Olor columbianus.*
[Trumpeter Swan. *Olor buccinator.*
Canada Goose. *Branta canadensis.*
[Brant. *Branta bernicla.*
Barnacle Goose. *Branta leucopsis.*
White-fronted Goose. *Anser albifrons.*

103

Snow Goose. *Chen caerulescens.*
Ross's Goose. *Chen rossii.*
[Fulvous Whistling Duck. *Dendrocygna bicolor.*
Mallard. *Anas platyrhynchos.*
Black Duck. *Anas rubripes.*
Mottled Duck. *Anas fulvigula.*
Gadwall. *Anas strepera.*
Pintail. *Anas acuta.*
Green-winged Teal. *Anas crecca.*
Blue-winged Teal. *Anas discors.*
Cinnamon Teal. *Anas cyanoptera.*
Northern Shoveller. *Anas clypeata.*
[European Wigeon. *Anas penelope.*
American Wigeon. *Anas americana.*
Wood Duck. *Aix sponsa.*
Redhead. *Aythya americana.*
Ring-necked Duck. *Aythya collaris.*
Canvasback. *Aythya valisineria.*
Greater Scaup. *Aythya marila.*
Lesser Scaup. *Aythya affinis.*
Common Goldeneye. *Bucephala clangula.*
[Barrow's Goldeneye. *Bucephala islandica.*
Bufflehead. *Bucephala albeola.*
Oldsquaw. *Clangula hyemalis.*
White-winged Scoter. *Melanitta deglandi.*
Surf Scoter. *Melanitta perspicillata.*
[Black Scoter. *Melanitta nigra.*
Ruddy Duck. *Oxyura jamaicensis.*
Hooded Merganser. *Lophodytes cucullatus.*
Common Merganser. *Mergus merganser.*
Red-breasted Merganser. *Mergus serrator.*
Turkey Vulture. *Cathartes aura.*
Black Vulture. *Coragyps atratus.*
White-tailed Kite. *Elanus leucurus.*
Swallow-tailed Kite. *Elanoides forficatus.*
Mississippi Kite. *Ictinia mississippiensis.*
Goshawk. *Accipiter gentilis.*
Sharp-shinned Hawk. *Accipiter striatus.*
Cooper's Hawk. *Accipiter cooperii.*
Red-tailed Hawk. *Buteo jamaicensis.*

Red-shouldered Hawk. *Buteo lineatus.*
Broad-winged Hawk. *Buteo platypterus.*
Swainson's Hawk. *Buteo swainsoni.*
Rough-legged Hawk. *Buteo lagopus.*
Ferruginous Hawk. *Buteo regalis.*
Harris's Hawk. *Parabuteo unicinctus.*
Golden Eagle. *Aquila chrysaetos.*
Bald Eagle. *Haliaeetus leucocephalus.*
Marsh Hawk. *Circus cyaneus.*
Osprey or Fish Hawk. *Pandion haliaetus.*
[Caracara. *Caracara cheriway.*
Gyrfalcon. *Falco rusticolus.*
Prairie Falcon. *Falco mexicanus.*
Peregrine Falcon. *Falco peregrinus.*
Merlin. *Falco columbarius.*
American Kestrel. *Falco sparverius.*
Greater Prairie Chicken. *Tympanuchus cupido.*
Lesser Prairie Chicken. *Tympanuchus pallidicinctus.*
[Sharp-tailed Grouse. *Pedioecetes phasianellus.*
[Sage Grouse. *Centrocercus urophasianus.*
Bobwhite. *Colinus virginianus.*
Scaled Quail. *Callipepla squamata.*
Ring-necked Pheasant. *Phasianus colchicus.*
Wild Turkey. *Meleagris gallopavo.*
Whooping Crane. *Grus americana.*
Sandhill Crane. *Grus canadensis.*
King Rail. *Rallus elegans.*
Virginia Rail. *Rallus limicola.*
Sora. *Porzana carolina.*
Yellow Rail. *Coturnicops noveboracensis.*
Black Rail. *Laterallus jamaicensis.*
Purple Gallinule. *Porphyrula martinica.*
Common Gallinule or Moorhen. *Gallinula chloropus.*
American Coot. *Fulica americana.*
Semipalmated Plover. *Charadrius semipalmatus.*
Piping Plover. *Charadrius melodus.*
Snowy Plover. *Charadrius alexandrinus.*
Killdeer. *Charadrius vociferus.*
Mountain Plover. *Charadrius montanus.*
American Golden Plover. *Pluvialis dominica.*

Black-bellied Plover. *Pluvialis squatarola.*
Ruddy Turnstone. *Arenaria interpres.*
American Woodcock. *Philohela minor.*
Common Snipe. *Capella gallinago.*
Long-billed Curlew. *Numenius americanus.*
Whimbrel. *Numenius phaeopus.*
Eskimo Curlew. *Numenius borealis.*
Upland Sandpiper. *Bartramia longicauda.*
Spotted Sandpiper. *Actitis macularia.*
Solitary Sandpiper. *Tringa solitaria.*
Greater Yellowlegs. *Tringa melanoleuca.*
Lesser Yellowlegs. *Tringa flavipes.*
Willet. *Catoptrophorus semipalmatus.*
Red Knot. *Calidris canutus.*
Pectoral Sandpiper. *Calidris melanotos.*
White-rumped Sandpiper. *Calidris fuscicollis.*
Baird's Sandpiper. *Calidris bairdii.*
Least Sandpiper. *Calidris minutilla.*
Dunlin. *Calidris alpina.*
Semipalmated Sandpiper. *Calidris pusilla.*
Western Sandpiper. *Calidris mauri.*
Sanderling. *Calidris alba.*
Short-billed Dowitcher. *Limnodromus griseus.*
Long-billed Dowitcher. *Limnodromus scolopaceus.*
Stilt Sandpiper. *Micropalama himantopus.*
Buff-breasted Sandpiper. *Tryngites subruficollis.*
Marbled Godwit. *Limosa fedoa.*
Hudsonian Godwit. *Limosa haemastica.*
American Avocet. *Recurvirostra americana.*
Black-necked Stilt. *Himantopus mexicanus.*
Red Phalarope. *Phalaropus fulicarius.*
Wilson's Phalarope. *Steganopus tricolor.*
Northern Phalarope. *Lobipes lobatus.*
Parasitic Jaeger. *Stercorarius parasiticus.*
Glaucous Gull. *Larus hyperboreus.*
[Iceland Gull. *Larus glaucoides.*
Glaucous-winged Gull. *Larus glaucescens.*
Herring Gull. *Larus argentatus.*
[California Gull. *Larus californicus.*
Ring-billed Gull. *Larus delawarensis.*

Laughing Gull. *Larus atricilla.*
Franklin's Gull. *Larus pipixcan.*
Bonaparte's Gull. *Larus philadelphia.*
Black-legged Kittiwake. *Rissa tridactyla.*
Sabine's Gull. *Xema sabini.*
Forster's Tern. *Sterna forsteri.*
Common Tern. *Sterna hirundo.*
[Roseate Tern. *Sterna dougallii.*
Least Tern. *Sterna albifrons.*
Caspian Tern. *Sterna caspia.*
Black Tern. *Chlidonias niger.*
Black Skimmer. *Rynchops nigra.*
Band-tailed Pigeon. *Columba fasciata.*
Rock Dove. *Columba livia.*
[White-winged Dove. *Zenaida asiatica.*
Mourning Dove. *Zenaida macroura.*
Passenger Pigeon. *Ectopistes migratorius.*
Ground Dove. *Columbina passerina.*
Inca Dove. *Scardafella inca.*
Carolina Parakeet. *Conuropsis carolinensis.*
[Monk Parakeet. *Myiopsitta monachus.*
Yellow-billed Cuckoo. *Coccyzus americanus.*
Black-billed Cuckoo. *Coccyzus erythropthalmus.*
Roadrunner. *Geococcyx californianus.*
Groove-billed Ani. *Crotophaga sulcirostris.*
Barn Owl. *Tyto alba.*
Screech Owl. *Otus asio.*
Great Horned Owl. *Bubo virginianus.*
Snowy Owl. *Nyctea scandiaca.*
Burrowing Owl. *Athene cunicularia.*
Barred Owl. *Strix varia.*
Long-eared Owl. *Asio otus.*
Short-eared Owl. *Asio flammeus.*
Saw-whet Owl. *Aegolius acadicus.*
Chuck-will's widow. *Caprimulgus carolinensis.*
Whip-poor-will. *Caprimulgus vociferus.*
Poor-will. *Phalaenoptilus nuttallii.*
Common Nighthawk. *Chordeiles minor.*
Lesser Nighthawk. *Chordeiles acutipennis.*
Chimney Swift. *Chaetura pelagica.*

107

[White-throated Swift. *Aeronautes saxatalis.*
Ruby-throated Hummingbird. *Archilochus colubris.*
Black-chinned Hummingbird. *Archilochus alexandri.*
Anna's Hummingbird. *Calypte anna.*
[Broad-tailed Hummingbird. *Selasphorus platycercus.*
Rufous Hummingbird. *Selasphorus rufus.*
[Calliope Hummingbird. *Stellula calliope.*
Belted Kingfisher. *Megaceryle alcyon.*
Common Flicker. *Colaptes auratus.*
Pileated Woodpecker. *Dryocopus pileatus.*
Red-bellied Woodpecker. *Melanerpes carolinus.*
Golden-fronted Woodpecker. *Melanerpes aurifrons.*
Red-headed Woodpecker. *Melanerpes erythrocephalus.*
Acorn Woodpecker. *Melanerpes formicivorus.*
Lewis's Woodpecker. *Melanerpes lewis.*
Yellow-bellied Sapsucker. *Sphyrapicus varius.*
Williamson's Sapsucker. *Sphyrapicus thyroideus.*
Hairy Woodpecker. *Picoides villosus.*
Downy Woodpecker. *Picoides pubescens.*
Ladder-backed Woodpecker. *Picoides scalaris.*
Red-cockaded Woodpecker. *Picoides borealis.*
[Ivory-billed Woodpecker. *Campephilus principalis.*
Eastern Kingbird. *Tyrannus tyrannus.*
Western Kingbird. *Tyrannus verticalis.*
Cassin's Kingbird. *Tyrannus vociferans.*
Scissor-tailed Flycatcher. *Muscivora forficata.*
Great Crested Flycatcher. *Myiarchus crinitus.*
Ash-throated Flycatcher. *Myiarchus cinerascens.*
Eastern Phoebe. *Sayornis phoebe.*
Say's Phoebe. *Sayornis saya.*
Yellow-bellied Flycatcher. *Empidonax flaviventris.*
Acadian Flycatcher. *Empidonax virescens.*
Willow Flycatcher. *Empidonax traillii.*
Alder Flycatcher. *Empidonax alnorum.*
Least Flycatcher. *Empidonax minimus.*
Hammond's Flycatcher. *Empidonax hammondii.*
Dusky Flycatcher. *Empidonax oberholseri.*
Western Flycatcher. *Empidonax difficilis.*
Eastern Wood Pewee. *Contopus virens.*
Western Wood Pewee. *Contopus sordidulus.*

Olive-sided Flycatcher. *Nuttallornis borealis.*
Vermilion Flycatcher. *Pyrocephalus rubinus.*
Horned Lark. *Eremophila alpestris.*
[Violet-green Swallow. *Tachycineta thalassina.*
Tree Swallow. *Iridoprocne bicolor.*
Bank Swallow. *Riparia riparia.*
Rough-winged Swallow. *Stelgidopteryx ruficollis.*
Barn Swallow. *Hirundo rustica.*
Cliff Swallow. *Petrochelidon pyrrhonota.*
Purple Martin. *Progne subis.*
Blue Jay. *Cyanocitta cristata.*
Steller's Jay. *Cyanocitta stelleri.*
Scrub Jay. *Aphelocoma coerulescens.*
Black-billed Magpie. *Pica pica.*
Common Raven. *Corvus corax.*
White-necked Raven. *Corvus cryptoleucus.*
Common Crow. *Corvus brachyrhynchos.*
Fish Crow. *Corvus ossifragus.*
Pinyon Jay. *Gymnorhinus cyanocephalus.*
Clark's Nutcracker. *Nucifraga columbiana.*
Black-capped Chickadee. *Parus atricapillus.*
Carolina Chickadee. *Parus carolinensis.*
Mountain Chickadee. *Parus gambeli.*
Tufted Titmouse. *Parus bicolor.*
Plain Titmouse. *Parus inornatus.*
Verdin. *Auriparus flaviceps.*
Bushtit. *Psaltriparus minimus.*
White-breasted Nuthatch. *Sitta carolinensis.*
Red-breasted Nuthatch. *Sitta canadensis.*
Brown-headed Nuthatch. *Sitta pusilla.*
Pygmy Nuthatch. *Sitta pygmaea.*
Brown Creeper. *Certhia familiaris.*
House Wren. *Troglodytes aedon.*
Winter Wren. *Troglodytes troglodytes.*
Bewick's Wren. *Thryomanes bewickii.*
Carolina Wren. *Thryothorus ludovicianus.*
Long-billed Marsh Wren. *Cistothorus palustris.*
Short-billed Marsh Wren. *Cistothorus platensis.*
Canyon Wren. *Catherpes mexicanus.*
Rock Wren. *Salpinctes obsoletus.*

Mockingbird. *Mimus polyglottos.*
Gray Catbird. *Dumetella carolinensis.*
Brown Thrasher. *Toxostoma rufum.*
Curve-billed Thrasher. *Toxostoma curvirostre.*
Sage Thrasher. *Oreoscoptes montanus.*
American Robin. *Turdus migratorius.*
Wood Thrush. *Hylocichla mustelina.*
Hermit Thrush. *Catharus guttatus.*
Swainson's Thrush. *Catharus ustulatus.*
Gray-cheeked Thrush. *Catharus minimus.*
Veery. *Catharus fuscescens.*
Eastern Bluebird. *Sialia sialis.*
Western Bluebird. *Sialia mexicana.*
Mountain Bluebird. *Sialia currucoides.*
Townsend's Solitaire. *Myadestes townsendi.*
Blue-gray Gnatcatcher. *Polioptila caerulea.*
Golden-crowned Kinglet. *Regulus satrapa.*
Ruby-crowned Kinglet. *Regulus calendula.*
Water Pipit. *Anthus spinoletta.*
Sprague's Pipit. *Anthus spragueii.*
Bohemian Waxwing. *Bombycilla garrulus.*
Cedar Waxwing. *Bombycilla cedrorum.*
Northern Shrike. *Lanius excubitor.*
Loggerhead Shrike. *Lanius ludovicianus.*
Starling. *Sturnus vulgaris.*
Black-capped Vireo. *Vireo atricapillus.*
White-eyed Vireo. *Vireo griseus.*
Bell's Vireo. *Vireo bellii.*
Gray Vireo. *Vireo vicinior.*
Yellow-throated Vireo. *Vireo flavifrons.*
Solitary Vireo. *Vireo solitarius.*
Red-eyed Vireo. *Vireo olivaceus.*
Philadelphia Vireo. *Vireo philadelphicus.*
Warbling Vireo. *Vireo gilvus.*
Black-and-White Warbler. *Mniotilta varia.*
Prothonotary Warbler. *Protonotaria citrea.*
Swainson's Warbler. *Limnothlypis swainsonii.*
Worm-eating Warbler. *Helmitheros vermivorus.*
Golden-winged Warbler. *Vermivora chrysoptera.*
Blue-winged Warbler. *Vermivora pinus.*

Tennessee Warbler. *Vermivora peregrina.*
Orange-crowned Warbler. *Vermivora celata.*
Nashville Warbler. *Vermivora ruficapilla.*
Virginia's Warbler. *Vermivora virginiae.*
Northern Parula Warbler. *Parula americana.*
Yellow Warbler. *Dendroica petechia.*
Magnolia Warbler. *Dendroica magnolia.*
Cape May Warbler. *Dendroica tigrina.*
Black-throated Blue Warbler. *Dendroica caerulescens.*
Yellow-rumped Warbler. *Dendroica coronata.*
Black-throated Gray Warbler. *Dendroica nigrescens.*
Townsend's Warbler. *Dendroica townsendi.*
Black-throated Green Warbler. *Dendroica virens.*
Cerulean Warbler. *Dendroica cerulea.*
Blackburnian Warbler. *Dendroica fusca.*
Yellow-throated Warbler. *Dendroica dominica.*
Chestnut-sided Warbler. *Dendroica pensylvanica.*
Bay-breasted Warbler. *Dendroica castanea.*
Blackpoll Warbler. *Dendroica striata.*
Pine Warbler. *Dendroica pinus.*
Prairie Warbler. *Dendroica discolor.*
Palm Warbler. *Dendroica palmarum.*
Ovenbird. *Seiurus aurocapillus.*
Northern Waterthrush. *Seiurus noveboracensis.*
Louisiana Waterthrush. *Seiurus motacilla.*
Kentucky Warbler. *Oporornis formosus.*
Connecticut Warbler. *Oporornis agilis.*
Mourning Warbler. *Oporornis philadelphia.*
MacGillivray's Warbler. *Oporornis tolmiei.*
Common Yellowthroat. *Geothlypis trichas.*
Yellow-breasted Chat. *Icteria virens.*
Hooded Warbler. *Wilsonia citrina.*
Wilson's Warbler. *Wilsonia pusilla.*
Canada Warbler. *Wilsonia canadensis.*
American Redstart. *Setophaga ruticilla.*
House Sparrow. *Passer domesticus.*
Bobolink. *Dolichonyx oryzivorus.*
Eastern Meadowlark. *Sturnella magna.*
Western Meadowlark. *Sturnella neglecta.*
Yellow-headed Blackbird. *Xanthocephalus xanthocephalus.* 111

Red-winged Blackbird. *Agelaius phoeniceus.*
Orchard Oriole. *Icterus spurius.*
Northern Oriole. *Icterus galbula.*
Rusty Blackbird. *Euphagus carolinus.*
Brewer's Blackbird. *Euphagus cyanocephalus.*
Great-tailed Grackle. *Quiscalus mexicanus.*
Common Grackle. *Quiscalus quiscula.*
Brown-headed Cowbird. *Molothrus ater.*
Western Tanager. *Piranga ludoviciana.*
Scarlet Tanager. *Piranga olivacea.*
Summer Tanager. *Piranga rubra.*
Cardinal. *Cardinalis cardinalis.*
Pyrrhuloxia. *Cardinalis sinuatus.*
Rose-breasted Grosbeak. *Pheucticus ludovicianus.*
Black-headed Grosbeak. *Pheucticus melanocephalus.*
Blue Grosbeak. *Guiraca caerulea.*
Indigo Bunting. *Passerina cyanea.*
Lazuli Bunting. *Passerina amoena.*
Painted Bunting. *Passerina ciris.*
Dickcissel. *Spiza americana.*
Evening Grosbeak. *Hesperiphona vespertina.*
Purple Finch. *Carpodacus purpureus.*
Cassin's Finch. *Carpodacus cassinii.*
House Finch. *Carpodacus mexicanus.*
Common Redpoll. *Carduelis flammea.*
Pine Siskin. *Carduelis pinus.*
American Goldfinch. *Carduelis tristis.*
Lesser Goldfinch. *Carduelis psaltria.*
Red Crossbill. *Loxia curvirostra.*
White-winged Crossbill. *Loxia leucoptera.*
Green-tailed Towhee. *Pipilo chlorurus.*
Rufous-sided Towhee. *Pipilo erythrophthalmus.*
Brown Towhee. *Pipilo fuscus.*
Lark Bunting. *Calamospiza melanocorys.*
Savannah Sparrow. *Passerculus sandwichensis.*
Grasshopper Sparrow. *Ammodramus savannarum.*
Baird's Sparrow. *Ammodramus bairdii.*
Henslow's Sparrow. *Ammodramus henslowii.*
Sharp-tailed Sparrow. *Ammospiza caudacuta.*
Le Conte's Sparrow. *Ammospiza leconteii.*

Vesper Sparrow. *Pooecetes gramineus.*
Lark Sparrow. *Chondestes grammacus.*
Rufous-crowned Sparrow. *Aimophila ruficeps.*
Bachman's Sparrow. *Aimophila aestivalis.*
Cassin's Sparrow. *Aimophila cassinii.*
Black-throated Sparrow. *Amphispiza bilineata.*
Dark-eyed Junco. *Junco hyemalis.*
Gray-headed Junco. *Junco caniceps.*
Tree Sparrow. *Spizella arborea.*
Chipping Sparrow. *Spizella passerina.*
Clay-colored Sparrow. *Spizella pallida.*
Brewer's Sparrow. *Spizella breweri.*
Field Sparrow. *Spizella pusilla.*
Harris's Sparrow. *Zonotrichia querula.*
White-crowned Sparrow. *Zonotrichia leucophrys.*
White-throated Sparrow. *Zonotrichia albicollis.*
Fox Sparrow. *Passerella iliaca.*
Lincoln's Sparrow. *Melospiza lincolnii.*
Swamp Sparrow. *Melospiza georgiana.*
Song Sparrow. *Melospiza melodia.*
McCown's Longspur. *Calcarius mccownii.*
Lapland Longspur. *Calcarius lapponicus.*
Smith's Longspur. *Calcarius pictus.*
Chestnut-collared Longspur. *Calcarius ornatus.*
Snow Bunting. *Plectrophenax nivalis.*